Intent to Sell

Marketing the Genre Novel

BY JEFFREY A. MARKS

ISBN:

ISBN-13: 978-1470102555

ISBN-10: 1470102552

First Book printing 2001

Second Printing 2005

Third Printing 2010

Fourth Printing 2012

Manufactured in the United States of America

10 9 8 7 6 5 4 3 2 1

Cover design: Patty G. Henderson

Table of Contents

Acknowledgements

I've been engaged in a learning process of how to promote your own work for almost 15 years now. I'm going to try to thank the people who have been instrumental in teaching me these skills, but of course, over such a period of time it's nearly impossible to remember all the mentors and helpers along the way.

My first experiences in booksignings came from helping Deborah Adams and Steven Womack set up a Midwest tour. I never had such problems, but I learned an invaluable amount from each of them. The same goes for Joan Hess, and Sharyn McCrumb who came through Ohio on a tour before my first book collection came out. I learned more spending the day with them than I did from any book or conference.

My friends, Kate Stine and Keith Kahla, have let me pick their brains about a million different ideas. They are a storehouse of advice and help in knowing what works and what doesn't.

Of course, my education has come from MurderMustAdvertise, the Yahoo group that I've moderated for ten year now, and from Kate Derie who gave me the opportunity to lead that group. Most of the ideas in this book have come from that group and their long hours of trial and error.

A tip of the hat to Jeff Caywood, my first publicity assistant who showed me the need for organization and the power of what good spreadsheets and word processors can do. Eleven books later I'm still using some of the techniques he showed me.

My family and friends have been most supportive throughout my career. My partner, Tony, parents, my sister, and my nephews all make allowance for my erratic schedule and hours chained to the computer. My friends are helpful and encouraging, asking about my latest books and promoting my works in their lives. My family and friends are what it's all about.

Chapter 1
Book Promotions

When I started writing professionally, I envied the authors who had followed a more traditional undergraduate educational program, studying English, and then completing an MFA in creative writing. My education had nothing to do with literature. I'd gone the business route in hopes of earning a respectable living — an undergraduate degree in computers and a MBA from a local university. Those degrees didn't seem to be much help when I began writing. For several years, I practiced my writing skills before I could craft a story worth reading. I despaired that I'd wasted my college career.

Yet, when I did start publishing, I realized that I'd obtained a very valuable education. During the course of that master's degree, I'd done consulting work with small businesses, especially in the area of business marketing. When my first book appeared on the shelves, I realized how on my own I really was. Hundreds of thousands of titles are published each year, and I was only one of them.

So I began using my marketing skills to promote my books. Despite my passion for the written word, I knew that publishers considered my masterpiece to be another product to be sold. Even with the sales reps and publicist, I knew that I was the best tool I possessed for selling my books. So I decided to put that tool in action.

I looked at my writing career as a small business and applied the same sorts of principles to it as I would to any of my consulting clients. First, know that you're not likely to make any money from this commodity any time soon. Most new businesses don't generate a profit in the first four to five years of operation. In the beginning, companies need outside capitalization in order to make ends meet. I'm not advocating that you sell your children and cash in your retirement to be an author. Never spend more than you can afford to lose. It applies to gambling, and it holds for publishing as well. However, you should take a long hard look at what your salary will allow, and include marketing as a part of the family budget. There are lots of cheap and free promotions that can be done in the name of marketing. Not everything is television commercials and billboards. In fact, those are two of the least productive selling techniques to use. We'll talk about all of those during the course of the book.

When I received the advance for my first book, I invested the money into promotions. I've known myriad authors who have spent their advances on cars, appliances, or to quit their day job. Then when they realize that book promotions require a certain amount of cash, they have to dip into their own pocketbooks. By then the window of opportunity might be closed for the book. That's the reality of publishing. You'll need to promote yourself. No one is as committed or concerned about your career as you are. So you'll be your number one resource in making your book sell thousands of copies.

Another thing to remember is that most start-up businesses fail in the first years of operation. We don't want that to happen to you. In publishing, it's not bankruptcy court that looms, but poor sales figures, large numbers of remaindered books, and low sell-throughs. You'll need to know what these terms mean and how to prevent them. In some cases, bookstores, distributors, and warehouse stores as well as the publishing house have a voice in who gets published. No one in the industry wants to carry books that don't sell. You'll have to make sure that your career progresses in the right direction.

In bringing your writing dreams to fruition, you'll first need to set some goals for your career. What do you hope to achieve with the publication of your book? You'll need to be precise and concise. Don't decide, "I want to be a best-seller" or "I want to make millions of dollars." That's entirely too generic. Rather you should say, "I want to reach number five on the *New York Times* Bestsellers List" or "I want to sell 10,000 copies of my book." For my first novel, I selected a goal of selling the entirety of my first printing in less than one year. Not a ridiculously ambitious goal, but one that would make my publisher see that I was dedicated to the books and to my future as a writer. So I found out what my print run was, and decided how to proceed to make this happen. Your goals should be relatively short-term (less than a year) and specific.

From those origins, you'll need to look at what steps to take to realize these goals. If you've set a very ambitious bar for yourself, you'll need to invest more money and time to make that happen. If you're only looking to sell 100 copies of your book, well, you can pretty much do that with your hands strapped behind your back and your wallet tucked in your pocket.

So without the expectation of quick profits and maddening crowds at your every signing, you'll need to get to work — and work it is. You'll spend hours sweating and brainstorming about how to get your book in front of millions of people. It's enough to make sure people know who you are and what your book is about. Word of mouth about the quality of your book should take it from there.

You need to find a way to make your book conspicuous. It can be done. Authors do it all the time. Sometimes with the help of their publishers, but many times without any assistance. Nothing beats a well-written book as a product. Just as no amount of advertising dollars will sell Chia Pets, a poorly written book won't have the word-of-mouth sales that you need to generate interest in your novel.

This book isn't going to teach you how to write the Great American Novel (we'll assume you've already finished that task!), but it will give you some ideas and pointers on how to best market that book in today's publishing environment. Using this book, you should be able to come up with a complete marketing plan to best get your book noticed by bookstores, libraries, and readers who will be specifically interested in your works. For now, I'll just say congratulations, and best of luck in making your writing dreams come true.

While many books profess to help you sell books, nearly all of them are geared towards non-fiction which is much easier to market than genre fiction. *Intent to Sell* will cover mainly genre fiction in all formats, including eBooks, though some tips for selling genre non-fiction will be given as well.

The good news is that you have sold your book. Don't think that it's time to kick up your feet and relax, letting the royalties flow in like water down a hill. Publishing is a radically different industry than it was 20 years ago and even more in the ten years since the first edition of this book was published. I'm not going to debate the worth of the changes. We're being realists here. We're going to deal with the situation, as it exists today.

Most first-time authors still carry the mental picture of Ernest Hemingway, writing in a Parisian café and running with the bulls in Pamplona. Ernie didn't have to hawk his wares at the local strip mall. He was too busy experiencing life and gathering fodder for his next novel. Well, that was nearly a century ago. We don't romanticize Model A Fords and crank phones, but for some reason, we still conjure up the romantic images of the free-spirit author.

Hemingway wouldn't even recognize the publishing houses of today. Most of them have been consolidated into a few major multinational entertainment conglomerates. Major chain stores and big box stores dominate the landscape of bookselling as opposed to the smaller independent stores of 50 years ago. Today Amazon sells more books online than Barnes and Noble who in turn sells more books through its chain of stores than all the independent bookstores combined. Some estimates say that Wal-Mart can sell up to 50 % of a best-selling title. What does that mean to the writer? Plenty.

In terms of the merging publishers, there's been a shift in attitude from the "gentleman's business" of publishing to the concept of the book as a moneymaking commodity. Gone are the days of nurturing an author's career through three or four mediocre books until her potential is realized. Publishers want to see a profit on each and every book. If they don't see a profit, chances are that your career will be cut short, sometimes even after a single book. Sometimes, a bookstore chain's buyer or distributor rep will note the poor sales of a particular title and inform the publisher that books by the same author will no longer be stocked, negating any chance of future book deals. Such bans effectively force an author to undergo a name change in order to continue writing — like some sort of literary out-law—or to start fresh and begin a career in fast food. These facts make the job of properly marketing your book even more critical to your career.

As companies melded individual publishers into large conglomer-ates, the formerly independent publishing houses combined functions such as their publicity and marketing departments. The result is that fewer publicists handle more books. This means that your book will likely be one of 30 to 40 books that your publicist is handling at any given time. Even if you assume that the publicist puts in an eighty-hour workweek and all books are treated equally, that's two hours of time each week that can be devoted to your work. That's not enough time to set up a tour, or even telephone all the stores in your zip code.

While there are still certain duties that you should expect your publicist to perform, you'll have to shoulder a greater part of the publicity burden than in the past. Some authors have invested in public relations specialists to help them out. After all, these English majors didn't want to learn about business and marketing in college. Still be sure to keep your publisher and publicist informed about all of your efforts. Duplication of efforts helps no one.

It's been estimated that the average shelf life of a paperback book is around 43 days. Let's be honest — I've had loaves of bread in my refrig-erator older than that. What can you possibly do in six weeks to make sure that your book doesn't fall to the wayside like so many others? You have to take the time and effort to make your publication an event and a unique offering.

Ironically, while the number of New York publishers has de-clined, the number of books being published has actually increased. As the bigger houses merged, they reduced the number of titles published at their houses. In mystery, this left a number of mid-list authors suddenly without a publisher. Luckily, small presses saw this as an opportunity to sign up proven authors. While none of these authors would pen the next million dollar seller, the small presses knew that they would at least earn back their advance, if not more, from publishing books by talented, mid-list authors who were cut loose as a result of changes in the publishing industry.

An even smaller press has become available with the digital revo-lution. The home computer has made the Print-on-Demand and self-publishing industries boom. In times past, books not printed by a commercial publishing house were considered vanity titles. That's not the case anymore.

Desktop publishing has made it possible to do complete pre-press work in a home office, before sending a book to a printer. By being able to do so much of the publishing process from a home office, many people who could not have (or would not have) published with a major publisher can now produce a book. The costs are reduced and more authors can make a profit in this arrangement. Print-on-Demand and self-publishing create more competition for your title, and other books that consumers could buy. Add in the growing electronic book field, and you've got a real battle for the book dollars.

Even with the pressure of the increased competition, you'll need to walk that thin line between successful marketing and being obnoxious. You don't want to end up looking like "the telemarketer" of the promotional world. You plan to make writing your career, so you want to make a lasting impression, and make it a good one. There are authors who are notorious for their diva-like behavior, for hogging panels, badmouthing others, and practically forcing books on customers. You don't want that type of reputation. In a world as small as publishing, word spreads quickly.

In the beginning, it's difficult for an author to make the determination between what is acceptable and sensible self-promotion and obnoxious arm twisting. After all, every promotion opportunity seems pushy at first. However, people will give you a lot of leeway. You've done something that few people will do, and you've earned the right to crow about your success. So do so, then it's time to get down to work.

Chapter 2
Starting Now

So you've sold your novel. Congratulations. Now all you have to do is sit back and wait for the reviews and royalties to come rolling in, right? Not exactly. The process of promoting your own work should begin before the ink is dry on your contracts. I'm not going to talk about including promotional language in the contract with your publisher. That's the agent's job, if you have one. If not, that's the subject of an entirely different book.

For the most part, you're on your own with promotions. Don't sit back and expect your publisher to buy full-page ads in *Publishers Weekly* and *The New York Times*. The only time where the publisher will really start to invest in marketing your books is when they see a commitment from you to do the same. If they realize that you're giving this book your all, they are far more likely to offer you publicity in some manner. Some authors are able to get the publisher to commit matching funds to promotion, asking the publisher to spend one dollar of their budget for each dollar of your promotional money. This arrangement tells the publisher that you're more than willing to pay what is necessary — provided that they are as well.

So where do you begin in promoting your book? One of the first things you should start thinking about once you have a firm contract is blurbs. Blurbs or cover quotes are reviews found directly on the book's cover or on one of the first pages of the book. You've seen the quotes from authors that extol the virtues of a book. You, the author, solicit all of those comments.

So how do you go about getting these quotes? Don't be fooled. John Grisham and Stephen King are not waiting at home to read your manuscript. For that matter, most of the big names in any genre won't be either. They will be writing their own books. You have to remember that they have books that are due to their publishers as well. That's how they make their money, and that should be respected.

If that's the case, you need to make intelligent decisions about who to ask for quotes. The first logical step is to think of any authors that you've met or networked with in the recent past. If you attended a workshop taught by a name author, you might want to contact him for a quote. Once you start to know the ins-and-outs of publishing, you'll realize that personal connections often exist between the author and the blurber. It's natural to ask someone that you have a relationship with. They will be more likely to do it and to do a good job of providing a quote.

Once you've identified those familiar authors, then you'll need to do some analysis. The goal in gathering these quotes is to let your reader know what type of book you have written and that it is a good example of the subgenre that you write in. So if you write funny, genteel mysteries, you don't want to ask a hard-drinking PI writer to provide you with a cover quote. People will see the name and assume that you write the same type of book. You need to be honest with yourself in regard to what you write. While all of us want to think that we transcend the genres and write for all time, most of us will be categorized with other authors who write in a similar vein. Those are the people we need to seek out for quotes.

After receiving your first batch of cover blurbs, you still might need to contact more authors. If you can, you should write to five to seven authors and request a quote. This takes into account the fact that some of the authors will say "no," at the outset, while others will say "yes," but for some reason or another will be unable to complete the assignment. Hopefully, you'll still net three usable quotes for the cover out of your five to seven request. Give the authors at least six weeks to come up with a blurb. No wins when you pressure the person who is doing you a favor.

My first novel was a historical mystery with some light humor, set after the Civil War. I made a list of well-known authors who are tangentially associated with these topics. Authors who write about history, authors who write humorous mysteries, authors who are considered authorities on the Civil War. All of these are fair game for cover quotes.

What you won't see on my list are authors who write mysteries set around the Civil War. Why? I enjoy these authors' books, and count some of them among my friends. Aren't these authors very close to the type of book that I write? Yes, but they are *too* close. While I'm not advocating direct competition with other authors, I don't want you to establish a pecking order with you on the bottom rung. I do not want to portray myself as a lesser author in my chosen subgenera. Just like Puffs wouldn't ask Kleenex for a testimonial, I don't want other authors of this era put in the position of being "the authority" on the time period. So while I would gladly blurb someone else's Civil War mystery, I would not dream of asking another author of that subgenre to give me a cover quote.

From the list I created, I ended up with blurbs from a mystery author who writes about Medieval times, another mystery author who writes books set in the 1870s, and a third author who has written nonfiction works about the Civil War. This set of authors should give the reader an idea of what my book is about.

To this point, I've kept the discussion to requesting that authors give you quotes. For the most part, this is the norm. There are a few exceptions to this rule, but please use blurbs from other sources sparingly. Well-known booksellers, and editors of fan magazines can be used as cover quotes. After so many years in the genre, they can be expected to provide a knowledgeable opinion about the worth of the book. J.A. Konrath has used cover quotes from booksellers with great success.

Under no circumstances should you request a "reader" to give you a quote. In today's world, a person with a different last name doesn't imply impartiality in the review. The blurber could easily be your sister, mother or stepparent. Their opinion has no weight with the public and identifies you as an amateur. Unless the reader is readily identifiable as a celebrity, then this path should be avoided at all cost. Obviously, no one would argue with Oprah or Madonna offering a blurb, but try to avoid last year's Miss Dairy from your county fair.

When approaching an author to provide a quote, you should first send a letter. How do you find the address of the author if she is not a friend? First, query the web. There are a number of websites you can use to look up addresses. Likewise, look in the membership directory of Sisters-in-Crime or Mystery Writers of America for an address. It works the same for other genres. If the author is not found in any of sources you consult, then address the letter in care of the agent, provided you have that piece of information. Many authors will dedicate a book to their agent, so read the first few pages of the book to find that out. If that fails, send the letter in care of the author's publisher. Publisher information is readily available from websites like Amazon.com or the local library.

Never send a copy of the book as an opening gambit. It's presumptuous, not to mention expensive. A letter is appropriate at this point. The letter should explain that you have a book coming out and would like the author to provide a cover quote for the book. Your letter should give the title of the book, the publication date, and the date by which you would need the quote. Provide a SASE for the author. There's no reason to make the author pay for your request.

If the author assents, you'll need to make a copy of the manuscript and have it professionally bound. It can be as simple as putting a plastic cover and cardboard backing on it while having it bound with plastic rings. You just need to make sure that it's portable, and that the pages won't spill out. These are not terribly cheap, which is another reason for monitoring the number of blurbers.

Save the address information for the people you contact. You should put them in a word processing document or a spreadsheet. You'll need the addresses if you need to contact the author again for more information. Additionally, it is considered good-mannered to send the author a copy of the book when the book is released. They deserve that and more for helping you out.

Once the quotes have come back from the author, you'll need to accumulate them. Include them all on a single page with a title of "What People are Saying about My Book." Then each blurb should be added (in quotes) along with the author's name, and a short bio (10 words or less). "Author of Title A" is sufficient. This page can be transmitted to your publisher so that they can be included on the book's cover.

As you are beginning to see, getting to know the people in the writing profession is important, but don't limit that network to just authors. The next step that you'll need to do is more sweeping. In terms of networking, you'll need to figure out who you know in all the fields that might come up during the book promotion process. For right now, I'm talking about flesh and blood friends, not Facebook "friends." Like with every other venture, who you know plays a big part in getting things done.

I'm not encouraging you to cultivate people solely for what they can do for you, or wanting you to exploit your social circle. That type of behavior tends to backfire in the long-run. Still, in the course of your adult day-to-day life you will run into literally hundreds of people who work in fields related to bookselling and promotions. All of these people are valuable contacts that can help you at the time your book comes out. It's estimated that each person knows about 250 people through daily contact with them, so by the time you factor in the people that your network knows, it becomes literally thousands of people. And all of these people have a friend, relative or acquaintance in common with you.

Chances are that as a writer you love books. Hence, it's only reasonable that you'll meet people who love books as well. Anyone from a bookseller to people in local writers groups to librarians are all people who can play a hand in promoting your work. Booksellers and librarians are particularly important contacts for your first book. Their support is critical to success. Usually, if you know the person well enough to contact them, a bibliophile is more than happy to help you. After all, they're excited for your triumph, and they'll look forward to reading your book. If you want to make contact at this point, a simple postcard announcing the selling of your book to a publisher is sufficient. Until the book is out and you can talk to audiences at a signing, it's best not to call. Most booksellers and librarians won't set up a signing or event without the book in hand, and it will be months before the advanced copies are ready. Plus many places don't want to schedule events too far in advance. Things can change and cause problems.

Another networking opportunity will be the people in writers groups. You can always go to talk to writers groups about your writing and career. The largest part of good promotional work is getting your name out there and increasing the recognition of your name as a commodity. If the reader can't remember your name, it's difficult to order your book.

When you visit a writers group, let the group observe some of your promotional effort firsthand. You could buy them a copy of this book as a way of helping them. Many unpublished authors don't know what to expect from a book signing or how to go about setting one up. In this way, you're helping them to further their career as well as promoting your own work.

Anyone in TV, radio or print is a potential contact for you. When the book comes out, you'll want to contact the media to get interviews.

Again, you'd be surprised at how well this can work. A former boss of mine had a daughter-in-law who worked as a TV camerawoman; She helped me to get on the morning show at her station. Likewise, a TV news anchor spotted me selling copies of *Canine Christmas* at the mall while wearing a Santa's hat and asked me to do an interview.

Serendipity plays a role in finding people who can help you with your book promotions. After I announced my first book to the people that I worked with, one of the men there pulled me aside and told me that if I'd written a mystery, I needed to talk to his mother. I had visions of some little old woman who sat at home with her cats, reading mysteries. Boy, was I wrong. It turned out that his mother was the events coordinator for the largest independent bookstore in Southwestern Ohio. He gave me her number, and I was able to set up a booksigning. On another occasion, I was talking to the manager of a local bookstore. He mentioned the name of his district manager. Because of the unusual last name, I knew at once that the district manager had gone to junior high school with me. He's been an invaluable contact. You'll be amazed at the amount of information you'll be offered by friends and family who know people in bookselling. All of these people can be contacted about signings and media events.

At this point, I'm going to encourage you to start maintaining a database of contacts. You'll need more than one database, or spreadsheet. The first database should be a list of your contacts that might be professionally interested in your book deal. You should have their name, address, and phone number, fax number, title, and e-mail address, if they have one. In this manner, you'll be able to create labels, fax lists or e-mail lists for sending out announcements to this group of people.

"I use MS Excel to track my contacts," says Julie Wray Herman, the author of the *Three Dirty Women* series of mysteries. "I have printed out the bookstores and media contacts as I make them. I use different color index cards for each type of contact. Green for bookstores, yellow for media, purple for reviewers, etc. I have a list of correspondence on the back of the cards so that I know at a glance when I last mailed something to this person and what it was that I mailed."

A side note to this is a strong recommendation to attend any conferences or conventions in the time before your book is published. Plan to attend at least one convention—preferably more. Now is the time to take notes on what you'll be doing when your book reaches the public, so consider this a walk-through or a dress rehearsal for when your book is released.

Attend the panel discussions and observe the speakers. How do they dress for the occasion? Notice how they bring a copy of their book with them to place next to their nameplate. Watch for different speaking styles of the panelists. Which one works best for you? Are you the light and breezy storyteller or the more serious scholarly type? Is every answer a joke or does the author merely nod and agree with the other panelists? All of these things should be observed carefully. Once you see firsthand how authors handle panel discussions, it's not quite so unfamiliar to you anymore, and the fear dissipates. Once you've seen how it's done, you can do it too. Try to imagine how you would carry yourself during a public discussion. Realize that just because you'll probably be nervous at your first panel discussion, you still need to take the time to answer as many of the panel questions that apply to your work. Attending panel discussions at conferences and conventions before your own book is published is a great learning opportunity.

Another thing you'll want to do when you attend conferences or conventions is to buy a couple of paperbacks by different writers and have the authors autograph them. There are usually plenty of opportunities to meet authors and get books signed at conferences. The idea is to observe what makes each author unique in terms of his or her booksignings. How does the author greet you? Jeremiah Healy, a well-known private eye writer, shakes hands with each fan, and introduces himself. Others simply smile at you. Do they ask for your name or just sign their name? Do they include postcards or bookmarks in the book after they sign? Do they put ink stamps in the book? Is this something you'd like to do? Again, by seeing how such things work, you become more familiar with the customs and find out what suits you best.

While you're at the conference, make sure to visit the dealer's room. While you're buying those paperbacks to use for watching the authors, introduce yourself to the booksellers. Bookstores that cater to your particular genre are your best friends. Make sure that they know who you are. That doesn't mean to dun them, but be sure to say hello and talk to them briefly about your work. Tell them when your book comes out, and from what publisher. Collect business cards from all of the stores in the dealer's room and input all of them into your new database of contacts.

While I would encourage you to go and talk with fans of the genre, it's probably too early to make much impact on them at this point. They are being inundated with messages about which books to buy that are on the shelf, today. I'm not advocating being rude to fans or in any way ignoring their very important function in the genre. Soon these will be the very people you are pitching your book to, but for now, they probably won't be terribly interested in a book that's not due until six months from now. Telling them about a book that won't be out for another six months or a year could be counter-productive. Certainly not as good a use of time as talking to the booksellers.

Some of the conferences and conventions have a special time for authors to announce their upcoming first novels for interested fans. Malice Domestic hosts a new author event, sponsored by *Mystery Scene* magazine. These events might be one of the best ways to make you known to a large number of fans. So for the time being, talk to fans while you're eating, or sitting next to someone at a panel or in line for the booksignings, but don't worry about promoting your book to fans when the pub date is still relatively far away.

If your publisher has a reception or party at the convention, be sure to attend. You might think that you have nothing to contribute at this point, but you learn a lot from spending the time with the editor and the other authors. Now that you're a professional, you have the chance to pick up a lot of tricks of the trade by listening. People love to talk about themselves, and authors are people, too! What do the other authors say about signings? If you have developed specific questions over the course of the weekend, ask authors at the publisher parties for answers. You might even find someone to blurb your book at one of these parties. Authors so rarely congregate that you should use the opportunity to mine the wealth here.

When you're not gallivanting around the world to conferences and publisher dinners, do a similar exercise at home. The local bookstores will be one of your biggest supporters in selling your book. You should canvas the area to find out the best stores for signings and how events are typically handled at those stores. Be sure to offer to autograph books at the store to increase interest in your titles.

In determining which stores are considered the best, read your daily and weekly newspapers. Which stores frequently have signings? Where did Sue Grafton go for her last signing? When a national celebrity came to town, what store hosted his signing? You'll definitely want to make sure to cultivate that store. Most likely, they have an extensive mailing list and media contact list. That store has the clout to pull in more people for your signing.

Still there's nothing wrong with doing mall signings, especially for a first time author. We'll discuss how to set up booksignings in a later chapter, but for now, you should just take the time to get familiar with the bookstores in town. It doesn't hurt to go in and introduce yourself to the managers. Don't spend a lot of time doing that, as store personnel change on a regular basis, but it's good to stop by to let the stores know they have a local author.

Local bookstores will keep you in mind for any number of events. Not just an individual book signing for your opus, but also events dealing with topics related to your book, and any reading groups that meet at the store. That can include writers' workshops and some of the topics that are included in your book. Events that are not specific to your genre will net you readers that would be difficult to market to in any other venue. All of these early techniques can help you make valuable contacts and new readers for your coming book.

Chapter 3
Everybody Knows Your Name

After life settles down from the initial excitement of your sale, you'll need to get organized for the upcoming promotions. You'll need to look the part of a successful author. I'm not talking about a pipe and tweed jacket with elbow patches. I'm talking about business cards and the accoutrements of today's writer. At some point in the publishing process, you'll receive an ISBN (International Standard Book Number — a 13 digit number these days), and the cover art for your book. Both of these are key pieces to the next phase of the marketing process.

Now that you're going to be a published author, you'll need to know a few terms for succeeding in the book world. The terms "sell-in" and "sell-through" are frequently used in publishing these days. At this phase of the process, you'll be doing mostly "sell-in" marketing, which is marketing to increase the demand for the book from the bookstores to the distributors. So you are trying to get the word out to bookstores that your book will be out. Presumably this will lead to the bookstore placing orders against the distributors.

If one of the major New York publishers is releasing your book, then you can be assured that your sell-in rate should not be an issue. The chains will automatically order a certain quantity, based on the expected demand. However, if you're part of the ever-growing small publisher phenomenon, you'll most likely have to work harder on the sell-in marketing. Most of the chains will only stock your book on a store-by-store basis. This means that you'll have to focus your efforts on to the stores in your area and in places that either have good sales records for your type of book or have a tie-in to your subject. Your book won't be able to sell well if it's in the warehouse. No matter how much marketing you do.

At the current time, I'm in the process of calling all the stores in my immediate area to tell them that my new book is out. Shouldn't they already know about me? Maybe. The book was reviewed in the local newspaper on the book page, but I'm still calling every one of them. When the stores find out that I have a new mystery novel out from a small press, they'll order it. I might even go in for a signing. But since the chains don't immediately ship it to the stores, they might never think to request it specially without my call.

Sell-in marketing is becoming more popular these days. Authors meet with sales-reps, bookstore managers, and buyers for the chain – whoever is the person who places the orders against the wholesalers. The idea is two-fold. First, you should be impressing on the chains that you're going to do everything in your power to make your book a success. You want to show the determination and firepower in your publicity plan. List the signings, the advertisements, and any broadcast appearances you've scheduled. If the chains see that you're dedicated to this process, they'll be more likely to stock your title. It would mean bigger sales for them.

The other idea is to familiarize the buyers and store owners with your name. Since you want to write for a long time, you want the appropriate people to remember your name the next time they have a chance to order your books. The old adages regarding who you know and networking all apply to writing. Obviously, you'll sell more books if your novels are in the stores and you want to be a familiar quantity to the people who get the books in the stores.

The other term is the "sell-through" rate. This is the rate at which the book is sold by the bookstores to the end customers, the readers. This type of marketing occurs after the publication date, when the book is already in the stores. We'll discuss particulars of how to improve the sell-through later in the book. If your book has a high sell-though, it's likely to go into additional printings. If your book has a low sell-through, it's more likely to end up on the remainders table. Sell-though is considered a measure of consumer demand for the book. In one of those publishing-related quirks, a book with a print run of 2000 copies where 1900 are sold is sometimes considered a better book (at 95% sell-through) than a book with a run of 200,000 where 100,000 are sold (at 50% sell-through). Publishers and chains look at these numbers carefully, which means you should too. The importance of the number tends not to look at the total demand along with the statistic.

Having stressed the need for sell-in marketing, you need to get to work as soon as you can. The information you receive from your publisher is very important to the process. The ISBN will become one of the most important items of information about your book. If possible, memorize it. If you can't remember the 13-digit number, write it down on a slip of paper and carry it with you at all times. The ISBN is used as a reference number in almost every book-related computer application. Booksellers can place orders from it. Even Amazon.com uses it as a search option. While I don't want you to repeat it to customers like an infomercial phone number, you should include the ISBN on all marketing paperwork that you create.

The other thing you'll need is your cover art, the drawings that will make up your dust jacket. You'll either receive a copy of just the front of the book or in some cases, a copy of the entire book jacket, front and back. In either case, this graphic will help you make pleasing presentations.

One of the most popular promotional items right now is the postcard. The front of the postcard holds the artwork from the front cover the book. The back of the card has the normal white space for the address on the right half of the card. On the left side of the card where the salutations normally go, you include information about your book. At the very least print the publication date, the title and author, the ISBN, price, and a condensed version of the dust jacket copy. Ideally, the text on the card should tell the potential reader everything needed to make a purchasing decision.

It used to be a novelty to get postcards announcing an author's new book, but lately it seems like everyone is mailing them. The post office should be thrilled. I probably receive two or three postcards a week from authors who have purchased mailing lists. While the lists can specifically target mystery readers, I prefer certain types of mysteries. These marketing tools do not differentiate. So you'll be sending out cards to readers who are not interested. At a cost of a postcard stamp, and the printing costs of the cards, you're looking at about 30 cents per card these days. While that doesn't sound like much, it adds up fast. If you get 1000 names on a mailing list, that's $300 spent on cards. 5000 cards is $1500, a sum larger than you're likely to make from such a promotional campaign. Additionally, you'll find that the sheer volume of postcards sent these days make many readers pitch cards without a second thought.

Another way to distribute postcards is to use them to stuff the bag of goodies attendees receive at most conferences and conventions. If you're willing to give a particular number of cards to a conference, conference organizers will place your postcards in the freebie bags. The bad thing is that they'll also put the cards of every other author in the same bag. As I said before, postcards used to be a novelty. But when you have 40 authors who all are submitting materials, you end up with a bag full of cards.

Some conventions have tried to remedy this problem by limiting the cards that go in each bag. So you'll only submit cards for a fraction of the number of attendees — a cost savings to you. The conference will put your cards in every fourth bag, alternating with other postcards for the other bags. So while your message gets out, it is not going to reach as many people as it could. Even when conferences limit the number of postcards in freebie bags many people will still not look at them. For instance, I've seen people carefully tilt their bag into the trash to get rid of all the book promotion postcards while keeping everything else that came in the bag!

Most conferences and conventions have a table where promotional items can be set out for attendees to pick up if they are so inclined. This can prove a much better investment of time and money, because you're not marketing to hundreds of people who might not be interested in your particular book. The readers choose the cards and gifts that they are interested in.

You might find some better uses for the postcards than mass distribution. I know authors who will include postcards in their correspondence and even in their bills. Presumably, the addressed person has some connection to the author, and this is a quick way of announcing your book. Most postcards fit snugly into a business envelope, so drop one in with your telephone bill next time around. Distribute postcards to bookstores. Many bookstores will let you leave a stack of cards by the register. Also bring stacks of the postcards to your book signings and give the cards to anyone who seems interested, but isn't ready to buy a book yet. The postcards can serve as a reminder to that potential reader.

So how can you best get your postcards noticed? There are a few ways. Obviously, pleasing cover art will draw readers to your work, but in many cases you don't have any voice in the cover art. One thing you should do is make the card slightly different in size. By varying the card's width or height, the postcard will stand out in the crowd. A card that doesn't conform will draw the eye to it and make the reader look more closely.

The downfall of postcards is that other than announcing your book, the postcard has no other useful function. Granted you could fold it to shove under a shaky table leg, or start your grill with it, but postcards are designed to be read and then trashed. So you're spending money on what will be a fifteen second marketing experience. There should be better ways to get the reader's attention for longer periods of time.

What else can you to draw attention to your upcoming books? There are lots of promotional items that are available. One of the more popular is the bookmark. The bookmark will have the cover printed on the front (along with some colored background since the cover will not fit proportionally on a bookmark). The back will have the same types of information as the postcard. Unlike the postcard, the bookmark does have another purpose, and one related to reading books. So if the bookmark is being used, the reader is having the same marketing experience every time he opens the book. Compare that to the postcard that is normally discarded after one reading.

Another ploy is the old-fashioned recipe card. According to Edgar -winning author Frankie Bailey, "I printed up my recipe for the murder weapon in my book ("yummy balls") on a postcard that I could mail out or use as a give away at signings or just when anyone asks about the book. I find it much easier to offer someone a recipe card for a candy ball that I can swear is delicious than to simply hand them a bookmark. Of course, the recipe card has my book information on the reverse side. And I doubt that they are tossing the cards after they've made the recipe. So hopefully, they're seeing my name often enough for it to be reinforced." Again, cards that have alternate purposes are more likely to be preserved.

More practical items get a better response from readers and get more play for your money. One item that is not used much, but has a long shelf life, is a pad of notepaper. Just the normal 3"x5" pad can include a small graphic of the book's cover. The title and author can be placed next to the graphic, and the ISBN, price, etc can be run along the bottom of the sheet. Now consider that each pad is a marketing experience, and if a sheet of paper is used for a note, it's possible that several people could see the advertisement. I've seen piles of notepads fly off the promotional table because of their practicality. The more uses that a product has, the more likely the reader is to take one and keep it.

The marketing experience doesn't end with paper products. There are companies that do nothing but create promotional items for business-es. Since you're a small business, you should consider your options. The companies offer pens, mugs, golf accessories, desk implements, toys, re-frigerator magnets and more. Since most of these items are practical, the reader is more likely to take one and keep it. The down side is that most of these items are outside the realm of cost-effectiveness for you. If you're only earning two dollars in royalties per book, is it reasonable to spend five dollars for a single stoneware mug? Not likely, since the reader will most likely only purchase one copy of the book. As a rule of thumb, don't spend more than a quarter to half of the profits of a book's per book roy-alties on a promotional gimmick. You don't want to spend more than your net profit per each copy sold. Ballpoint pens can fall in the realm of cost effectiveness, but that is one of the few items in a typical business supplies catalog that make sense for you to consider.

One last printed item that is a must is the business card. Just as they are important to executives in the professional world, they are im-portant to authors as well. You won't put the graphic of the cover art on the card; it makes the cards too expensive. What you'll need is your name, the book title, ISBN, publisher, and price. Along with this information you'll need some type of contact method. If you just plan on trading cards with bookstore owners, reviewers, and librarians, feel free to put your home address and phone number. After all, these are like-minded people in your profession. But it can also be helpful to pass out cards to fans. If you opt to use this approach as well, you might want to consider only put-ting an e-mail address or fax number, the least intrusive methods of com-munication. Under no circumstances would you want to pass out cards to strangers with your home address and phone number.

You'll also want to think about putting QR codes on your busi-ness cards as well. QR codes, or Quick Response code, are those ubiqui-tous bar-code squares seen on many products these days. The codes are targeted towards smart phones which scan the bar-code and will automati-cally use the phone's browser to go to the URL encoded in the bar-code. As a result, you can create QR codes for your website, your book's site or a book-selling page on Amazon, Barnes and Noble or another book-seller.

If you're still in the pre-publication stages of your book, you can still use QR codes on your business cards to send people to like you on

Facebook or follow you on Twitter. Likewise, you can send people to an email sign-up webpage to build your list of potential customers.

If you do plan on passing out cards to potential fans, then you might want to consider a second set of business cards with limited personal information. Cards usually only cost about $30 per thousand, so this is a relatively easy way to promote your book. Additionally, people are conditioned to hold on to business cards, which can be good for the future marketing of the book.

Another cheap promotional method is to design personalized letterhead and envelopes. This can be done with most any inkjet or laser printer and any of the usual suspects in word processing programs. At the top of the page, put the graphic on the left-hand side and a banner across the top of the page with the title and author. The concept is similar to dropping postcards in your bills and correspondence. Every letter that goes out will announce your new book. The nice thing about this approach is not only will the personalized letters that you write to reviewers and bookstores carry the book's information, but every letter you send will as well. It's almost an unconscious type of marketing.

If your cover is not available or you don't have a color printer, substitute clip art for the book's cover. Just make sure that the clip art is appropriate to the theme of the book and doesn't need explanation. For example, when *Canine Crimes* came out, I used clip art of an adorable mutt on all my correspondence. It related directly to the title of the book. Stay away from the more grisly images, such as skeletons, poison bottles, and skulls. You don't want to scare the letter readers.

The improvements made on the PC and the color printers have made graphics easy to create at home. Now you can get an assortment of items that can be loaded in your printer as book promotions. Consider that you can now create T-shirt iron-on stickers that you can print out of your computer. I've seen several authors create these shirts, emblazoned with the book's cover on the front of the shirt and a message such as "I'd rather be reading My Book Title" on the back. It's a great conversation starter and a way to introduce people to your work. Plus it's a walking advertisement, traveling anywhere that the owner does.

You can get a sheet of magnets as well. Just print the cover art from your book along with a catch slogan, and suddenly you have a message that you can put anywhere that has metal nearby. People routinely put magnets on their refrigerators, giving you an audience that might never come to a bookstore or read the book reviews in the newspaper.

For those of us who are too lazy to walk around wearing a T-shirt, there are always more modern modes of transportation. Joan Hess created a bumper sticker based on her successful Maggody mystery series. She had the messages printed up cheaply, and gave them out as promotional items as she signed books, and later via the Internet. Each of these will reach hundreds of people as the cars on the road. You should develop a catchy slogan so that the sticker will generate some discussions on what it means. "Read my book" might let people know that you're an author, but it hardly will get other drivers to ask about it if they think you've got a hard sell for them.

Similarly, I ordered license plates that say "DOG WRTR". Since my first two books were canine-related, it made a perfect opening for me to explain about my writing when people wanted to know the significance of the plates. Sharon Short, the author of the Josie Toadfern mysteries, uses "MRE RITR" as her plates. I've sold a number of copies of my books because of people asking me about the plates.

If you're not shy about promoting, you can put one of those large car door magnets on your vehicle. Home-owned businesses frequently use these to advertise home-repair businesses and their kind. No reason that you can't join the trend. You can get those printed up at a reasonable price (you'll never fit that one in your home printer!). Include the same information you do on your other printed publicity materials. It will likely be too difficult (or expensive) to get the book's cover printed on the magnet, so increase the size of the title, and your name on the sign. If you don't cause accidents from the people who turn their heads to read your sign, you'll be getting plenty of publicity from your car.

While you're considering what promotional materials to buy, you should also be scouting out the area for a few bookstores to work closely with. I have two or three booksellers in town that I know well, and who I rely on to carry my books from the day they are released. This is important because there are few things as frustrating as hearing that a friend went to a bookstore and couldn't find your book. You've lost a sale. If you know for a fact that Bookstore A always carries your book, point the potential reader to that store and tell them that you know they carry copies.

You'll want to select two or three stores to cement a relationship with. Once you've selected the stores where you want to direct people, shop there a few times, and introduce yourself to the manager. Keep in mind that bookstore personnel changes, so the management can change, too. Still, be pleasant to the current managers. Tell them about your book; ask about doing a signing at the store. After you get their name and the store's address, be sure to add them to your contacts spreadsheet. Invite the manager (and any store clerks you know) to your book launch party. Send them announcements about new books, awards, conferences, and any other newsworthy events. If you decide to create a newsletter, add them to the mailing list for that as well. Make sure they get Advance Reading Copies of your books.

If you can't get copies of your ARC from the publisher, either print up some of your own to give to the bookstore people or wait and give them a complimentary copy of the book once it comes out. Even if you do give your new bookstore sponsors an ARC, it wouldn't hurt to give them a signed copy of the finished novel if you can afford it. While it seems counter-intuitive to give away the product you are trying to sell, in some cases, "comping" (from complimentary copy) people the book can make good business sense. In the case of booksellers, most likely they're not going to buy a copy of the book when literally hundreds of titles are sitting around them every day. If you don't give them a complimentary copy, chances are that they will read it from the shelves without buying it. The same rule applies to librarians. Book reviewers should get free copies as well. They typically don't make enough money from reviews to afford the very books they read. The same holds true for certain authorities in your genre, and authors who you might want to curry favor with.

By building relationships with bookstores, you'll always have a few stores to point people to when they want to buy your book. The store will make extra sales, and so will you. For me, one of the stores I direct people to is the Barnes and Noble at Newport on the Levee in a mall in Northern Kentucky. The store always has my books in stock, and I know that anytime someone from that area says she can't find my books, I know that person will find them at that store.

Chapter 4
Electronic Business Card

Another requirement for authors in the information age is the author website. What was a novelty a decade ago is now a necessity. While many people will grumble about the additional expense of creating and maintaining a website, a well-designed page can be a huge help in your promotions. Many promoters feel that a web presence has replaced the brochure as a form of marketing.

You'll have to make a number of decisions before you go on-line. The first question with a website is what URL to pick. The URL is the name following "www." In my case, I selected JeffreyMarks.com as my URL. JeffMarks.com had already been selected, so that was out. Most authors I know use their name as the URL. Consider

www.krisneri.com,

www.evanovich.com,

www.suegrafton.com,

www.stevensaylor.com,

www.laurieking.com

and others. The benefit of this approach to naming is that the URL is simple to remember and reinforces the author's name. Even though ICANN (the ruling body for Internet naming conventions) has introduced new extensions such as .biz, .info, and .pro, .com is still the most popular of them and likely to stay that way. You should try to insure that your site has yourname.com as the URL. This is beneficial for when the reader decides to buy your book from a store. They should remember your name. You can find out if the name is available from a number of websites including www.register.com, www.godaddy.com, and www.networksolutions.com. If you have additional money, buy some of the other qualifiers and point them all to a single site for simplicity's sake. Try to reserve this early, so that no one buys it out from under you and tries to sell it back to you at a profit.

Another approach is to use a name associated with your books. Some authors use a book title as their URL. Others use a concept, such as Julie Wray Herman's www.mysterygarden.com for her gardening series, as the URL for their site. Such concept sites can be fine, but might not be as appropriate if your series changes or you decide to write a one-off book. You don't want to have to create a separate URL and web presence for each series or worse yet, each book. That would be too confusing for the reader to find a particular title's information.

If you have several books in a series, you might want to use the character's name as the URL. John Locke does this for his Donovan Creed series with the URL www.donovancreed.com.

Most sites are designed in a similar fashion. While the style and graphics might vary from author to author, the overall site layout is fairly consistent between sites. My site is rather whimsical and light-hearted. I write humorous books and I want the site to be warm and inviting as well.

My opening page, called the home page, has the latest news about my writing, information and links to what I'm working on now, and marketing tips that change monthly or more frequently.

My bio page has my photo on it along with some personal information. I do not include much information on my family. Just because I chose to write and be somewhat in the public eye, I don't believe I made that decision for all of my family. In many cases, I only mention my dog and a rough idea of where I live. I also include a page of Frequently Asked Questions (FAQs) that cover some interview topics that I'm growing tired of.

My books page has links to each of the books (which are all presented in a box above a short description of each title.) Each entry has the cover of the book, the price, publication date, and ISBN information along with a short clip on the book. Because I write in so many genres, I wanted to make sure it was easy to discern what titles were fiction or non-fiction.

It is becoming more difficult and expensive to produce your own pages. MS FrontPage is no longer offered as of MS Office 2007, which means spending more money for the software needed to develop a professional site. If you're a computer whiz, you have the skills to create the pages in Dreamweaver, ASP, or Cold Fusion, and you can probably figure out how to host your own website. If you have a friend or family member who can do the site for you, ask them to develop your web presence. Just remember that your updates will be done on their schedule, not yours if you need any updates. If you don't know any techies, there are a number of firms that will create a fully realized website for you and companies that will host your site. Most of this can be accomplished for under $400 and you'll have the ability to make back some of this cost in Internet marketing and sales.

Once you have the URL, you'll need to add graphics and text to the page. The graphics should include the cover of your book as well as a high-quality photo of the author. Kate Stine, the editor-in-chief and co-publisher of *Mystery Scene* Magazine, explains some of the things that busy editors look for.

"It's hard to believe how many hours of my life have been spent online searching in vain for information about authors we want to feature in *Mystery Scene* Magazine. So to make my life easier -- and your self-promotion more effective -- here is a list of items that should appear on every author's website.

1. Hi-res author photos and book cover shots —At least one of these photos should be a standard head shot. Wear solid colors, avoid clutter and soft focus shots, and make sure there's contrast between your hair and the background. Color images are fine, newspapers and magazines can convert them to black and white easily.

    Also include a variety of pictures in interesting settings and poses, some of which can tie in to settings or themes of your work: a racetrack, hospitals, banks, etc. Local settings are particularly popular with hometown papers. Add photos for each book, because editors won't run the same photos repeatedly.

    Be sure you understand what "hi-res" and "print quality" mean. These are large files that will reproduce well in print, not just look good on your website. As for credits and permissions, just a line saying the photo may be used for publicity purposes and a photographer credit, if any, is all that's needed.

    And here's a last tip: make sure the image file uses your last name. You'd be surprised how many photos are identified only by a string of numbers making it very easy to lose track of them.

2. A booklist —You should always have an up-to-date list of your books at your website. These can be arranged in several ways-- some authors like to have separate lists for their different series, for example, while others put that information in parentheses after each title in one big list. Whatever you do, make the chronological order of the series absolutely clear.

    Editors need as much advance time as possible to plan features so add forthcoming books as soon as you know the details.

    Create another list for short stories, including publication details (magazine, anthology, collections, etc.) and be sure to note if they feature your series characters.

Create yet another list if you've published nonfiction articles that might interest readers --and editors, by extension. I always take note for *Mystery Scene* if a writer has a track record in this area.

3. Biographical information
   (a) A short bio: 50 to 75 words suitable for bookstore introductions, program books, etc. Make sure to mention the name of series, the detective and the title of latest book. Try to make this both lively and descriptive. (No plot outlines!) Editors can make good use of this to promote upcoming features about you.

   (b) A longer bio: Elaborate and add possible marketing points, particularly details such as where the book is set, profession of detective(s), where you live, went to school, Make this lively but informative. Write in the third person; use quotes from yourself if you want. Some authors rewrite the opening paragraphs for each new book or for specific uses. Note where you've lived, schools attended, any interesting or pertinent information about your profession or hobbies and other background material. (Hint: keep the dry material at the bottom of the page.)

   (c) A short "interview." Pose intelligent, informed questions about your work-and then answer them. If you note that the recipient has permission to reprint the interview, many smaller media outlets will run this interview as is. Although *Mystery Scene* wouldn't reprint the entire piece, we will sometimes excerpt an interesting or funny question and answer and run it alongside a book review.

4. What's New
   Here's a good place to list recent awards, tours, honors, speaking engagements, upcoming conventions, TV deals, etc. Make sure to note dates of each entry and keep this section current.

5. Contact Information
   There are many long discussions about the advisability of posting contact information online but there must be some way for the media to contact you or your publicist, preferably both. Email is the easiest. Most authors use a post office box or have mail sent c/o their publisher.

   (a) Your email, mailing address and/or telephone.

(b) Your publicist's name, email, mailing address and/or telephone. You can list the main switchboard for the telephone.

"Of course, there are many other items, that might interest an editor. Say, interesting quotes, a trivia quiz, a crossword using clues from your books, fun sidebar items ("How to catch a cardsharp," "Boston slang," "The best national parks/getaway cars/Civil War sites," etc.). Some authors post reading guides, past newsletters, and essays as well, but the five basics listed here will keep you covered in the media."

The text on the page, called content, should be divided by area of interest. The opening page should give an introduction to you as an author and your works. There are as many ways to do this, as there are novels out on the market right now. No one way is better or worse unless you've loaded the page with so many graphics that it takes years to bring the page up. (Don't forget that many people are still on dial-up as well. Allow them to skip flash introductions and the like.) Possible pages might include a biography page or sample question and answer page, a page dedicated to each title, sample chapters of your books, touring schedules, and more.

One of the things that make a website a place where readers will return is new content. If you consider an Internet news site, the information on the page changes several times a day, meaning that you have to return to keep current with the page's data. On the other hand, if you're lucky, you'll publish two books in a year. The reader will only need to visit your site twice a year to find out everything that's going on in your part of the world. That's why frequently updated sites get more hits than sites that are modified less often.

One way to pull in readers is the use of first chapters or excerpts on your site. You don't want to put the entire book on-line; no one will want to buy it if they can get the book for free. Still, just as many publishers put the first chapter of the next novel in the back of a book, put a teaser on-line in order to lure the readers. This can be an especially good marketing tool if you're a first time author. You're giving the reader a free taste of the product before they have to commit to a purchase. Like giving out complimentary copies of the book, putting out a part of your book on the Internet for free might seem like you're wasting your words, but it can help too. How many times have you seen a person in a bookstore who picks up a book and reads the first few pages? You certainly don't go over to him and snatch the book from his hands. So why would you care any more if he reads it on-line? Be aware, however, that readers can get confused and think that they've read, and more importantly purchased, a book when in fact they've only read that gratuitous first chapter. Also be sure to check with your publisher to ensure that this does not violate the terms of your contract.

You want a lot of hits on your site, and you want people to come back repeatedly, so you're going to have to add interactive qualities. Polls, games, contests, and things of that nature are considered interactive, because the person at the keyboard is "interacting" or inputting information into the site. This information, if used properly, can greatly increase your marketing presence. Your goal in incorporating interactive activities should be to collect e-mail addresses and names. From this information, you've extended your contacts to include a number of people who are interested in your writing. If you're not comfortable with this technology, you can simply add a link to send an e-mail to you, fill out a simple survey, or a request to send more information on your books to the requestor.

We'll be covering interactive techniques in the chapter, Advanced Marketing Techniques. In the meantime, just keep in mind that you'll want to be changing things on the page on a regular basis to keep it interesting and to keep fans coming back.

One technique that will continue to bring people in is making sure that you have links from your site to articles and short stories that you have written. If you've done any writing for magazines or newspapers, in most cases, that text is out in their on-line archives. Once you find the URL of the story, it's a simple matter to include that on your site as a way for readers to get a better idea of your writing style and themes. I have links from most of my major writing assignments as well as several of the short stories I've written. The idea is to keep people at your site with content, and give them reasons to come back to read the new works.

Janet Evanovich has a full-time webmistress in the guise of her daughter, Alex. Her site has been a major promotional tool for her. She gets two million hits a day from over 100,000 unique users. She gets all these people interested in her site by interactive utilities. She conducts polls, has message boards to communicate with the author, and holds contests to name books and more. All of these factors give people a reason to visit on a regular basis.

So how do you get people out to your site? Once you get your site operational, you'll start getting a number of offers to submit your website to the major search engines. My advice is that this is another task to perform yourself. There are aggregator sites that will submit your website to all the major portals. You'll be asked a few questions about what categories your site falls into. Once you answer the questions, the aggregator will submit your site to all the search engines for you.

Some search engines will ask for payment so that your site will be listed higher on the more generic listings. What this means is that, for a higher payment, they'll see to it that your site comes up as the first link if the Internet surfer types in "mystery" or "writer" or something else as innocuous in a search engine. Most of these services want about $100 for the privilege of submitting to all the various search engine sites on the Internet. However, some of the aggregator sites are free of charge, and those are the ones you should look for. They will submit your information for no charge, but will typically sign you up for a newsletter or add you to their mailing list.

You can rely on web crawlers or spiders to do the work, but in studies, it's been shown that even the most effective spiders only crawl over about 16% of the web. Web crawlers are automated scripts that pull relevant data from the Web in an organized fashion. This data is used to update search results on the major search engines and provide faster results for on-line searches.

Another option is to submit your site to each of the major search engines individually. While each site is different, most of the sites allow you to go down from the portal's main menu to the appropriate submenus until you hit the place where your site logically belongs. From here, there will be a link to click on to add your site to the page. This will put your site in the listings on that page, and add you to the search engine's keyword queries. While this takes a bit more time than using an aggregator, it is more precise than the generic keywords used by aggregator sites. Following is a list of the major search engines where you can list your website.

Major Search Engines

Google	www.google.com
Yahoo!	www.yahoo.com
AOL	www.aol.com
Ask Jeeves	www.ask.com
Bing	www.bing.com

An alternative way to have the search engines find you is to have meta-tags put in the HTML code itself. The person responsible for the coding of the site should include tags in the programming. The tags can include your name, the book title, and the genre of the book. These tags are then sought out by some search engines and included in future searches. Meta-tags are a nice way to get your site listed on search engines because it involves no effort on your part, but keep in mind it will often take several months to be located by search engines.

There are multiple types of meta-tags for your site. The first of these is the title tag that search engines give a high relevance to when searching the Internet. Description tags are, as named, used as descriptions for the site. Not all search engines use these tags. Finally, there are keyword tags, which are being dropped by some search engines for misuse.

These are tags that describe you, your book, and should include words like genre, writer, books, etc.

Trading links is also good for improving traffic to your site. Other authors are more than willing to connect their sites to yours via a link. Essentially you add a pathway to another author's site, and they reciprocate. It is often used for people to find like-minded material from the overwhelming amount of data on the web. Adding links is a very simple process as well, making it an easy way to improve the number of hits to your website. Studies of traffic patterns on the Internet have shown that the majority of traffic to a site come from related links rather than search engine results. This makes getting the proper links on your site more imperative. For mysteries, I'd suggest the sites www.stopyourkillingme.com and www.mystery-cozy.com.

Don't bother with the huge garish banner ads that appear on some websites today. While the efficacy of the banners has long been challenged, recent studies have shown that the average consumer only clicks on the banner when they lose control of the mouse and make a mistake. Not a good statistic to support banners. By forgoing the ads, you'll save time on the download of your site, which has been shown to be a factor in consumer desires for a website.

One last function that can help you with your site is the connection to on-line booksellers. By now, practically everyone has heard of Amazon.com and BN.com (the website of Barnes and Noble), the two major players in the Internet bookselling business. Still, there are quite a few others, including Booksamillion.com, and more. One of the ways to make the purchase of your book easier is to link directly to one of these sellers and to the page that displays your title. The easier it is to find your book on the web, the more likely people will make the purchase.

Besides the major players, Book Sense (www.booksense.com) now provides links to local booksellers that have your book. The Book Sense program requires a zip code from the purchaser, but comes up with local independent booksellers and their websites. This allows the purchaser to buy on-line or go to the bookstore in person.

Most of these sites have an affiliates program as well. This provides you with a certain percentage of sales based on click-throughs from your site. So if the fan clicks on a book on your site and goes to the bookseller, you get an additional payment of typically 1% to 5%. Some of these programs are in danger at the moment because of sales tax regulations at the state level. You'll want to ensure that your state does not require sales tax to be collected before you sign up.

You'll also want to take the time to update the page that displays your title with the on-line booksellers (On Amazon.com, this is located under Author Central page.) Internet booksellers put out only the bare bones basics on your book page. They will list the title, author, price, and possibly reviews from the major outlets (*Publishers Weekly*, *Kirkus*, etc.). There are many things you can do to spruce up the site. For starters add your cover art. As mentioned before, adding graphics to a screen increases its attractiveness. Add the blurbs from your reviewers, reviews from lesser magazines and newspapers. This helps the reader make up her mind to buy your book. That's a powerful incentive to add content to your page.

As far as the sales ratings for the various sites go, don't spend too much time worrying about the numbers. The rankings are a relative measure of how many copies a book is selling, but it's in relation to every other book in the Amazon.com database. It's tempting to get obsessive about your ranking versus other mystery authors, Pulitzer Prize winners, Nobel Laureates and others, but frankly, the numbers are not as representative of gross sales as you would think. If you want to obsess over numbers, call Ingram instead and keep an eye on the stock levels of your book at the various warehouses. Things are changing rapidly; with the introduction of e-readers, Amazon is quickly approaching a 50 percent market share. That gives you great incentive to spruce up your web-pages.

I do tend to get caught up in the Worldcat system, which is an aggregator of information from over 9000 libraries in the nation. It's a great way to track your library sales. It's not comprehensive by any means, but it's a good indicator of library sales. If you're associated with a university, the service is free. Most library websites also have a way to link to the system via your library card number.

Another way to promote your website on-line is to use a weblog, or more frequently called a blog. A blog is an on-line notepad that allows you as the author to write about anything and everything that you want. Technorati now estimates that over 70 million blogs are out there in cyberspace. So how do you make sure that you're heard above the din of the other 69,999,999? With more than two new blogs created every second, is it even possible?

There are currently blogs related to every possible subject under the sun. Two of the main types that have sprung to life are political blogs and celebrity gossip blogs. Both receive millions of hits per day and generate significant ad revenue for the blogger.

However, as an author, I'd hope that you avoid these two subjects. I have seen authors write about politics, but if your remarks are controversial, you're likely to turn off as many readers as you turn on. That's not to say that you shouldn't speak your mind, but be respectful and keep your audience in mind.

Many authors feel that blogs are a wonderful way to connect on a more personal level with your readers. If you want to engage your readers in a discussion about what's important to you, then a blog is definitely the way to do it. It's personal, and if you allow comments on the site, you'll be able to communicate with your audience personally. However, for some, the workings of the author's mind are not of interest, and they are not going to appreciate the efforts made to display those workings to the world.

First, you need to make sure that you link your blog to other blogs in your genre. There are other authors doing the same thing that you are, and sharing links is just one way for both of you to get noticed. Swap links with your author website as well.

There are a number of blog search engines and directories where you can list your blog as well. ReadaBlog, Blogarama, BlogDex, Blog Universe, and more will all submit your blog to the search engines. As with the meta-tags on your website, be sure to have a precise title and keywords when submitting to these search engines. The right keywords will get your blog noticed by the right people.

You can also post announcements about the blog on various Usenet groups, YahooGroups, Kindleboards, Barnes and Noble's book club, Facebook, and forums. Not only announce that your blog has been launched, but you can also post announcements when you've written about a topic of interest. Do not post to the forums every time you write a blog entry. People will get annoyed and stop paying attention to the announcements.

Many people are now discussing whether blogs are worth the effort. If you have a day job or other commitments, do you really want to spend 30 minutes to produce 500 words on your daily thought —or is that time better spent writing your next novel?

Some authors have significantly curtailed their blog efforts once the original excitement of the new promotional tool wore off. Instead of posting daily or multiple times daily, they now post 2-3 times a week. They include guest bloggers and experts who can write about a particular subject. Some bloggers write one blog and post it in a variety of forums. All of these techniques are all designed to reduce the amount of time the author is spending writing a blog and not a new novel.

According to Heather Webber, the author of the Nina Quinn mystery series, "In blogging, finding the right balance of how often to post is simply trial by fire. In my experience, when I was blogging with two different group blogs, I found I quickly ran out of the creative steam needed to write essays twice a week. I'm down to blogging once a week and sometimes it's still too much--which is when it's good to have guest-bloggers on stand-by. In personal blogs, usually updated daily, I find people often have short posts mixed with longer ones, newsy items paired with essays, so there is a lot more leeway and freedom if you're on your own, but also a lot more responsibility."

One of the ways I've reduced my own involvement in blogging is by becoming one of five authors who writes for a particular site. I do the Friday posts on The Little Blog of Murder (www.thelittleblogofmurder.com.) In this way, I'm only writing one day a week for the blog, which significantly reduces my efforts in blogging. I can manage one day a week with my posting to talk about things that are going on in my life or with my writing. I've written about my health, my dogs, my family, my school, and my book collection. The five of us agreed that we would not include politics or controversy on our site. We wanted to sell books, not generate controversy surrounding us. Some sites don't have those rules, and I've seen Republican rants and posts of a sexual nature that would make your grandmother blush. While these sites might get more hits than discussions about the dog, I'm not sure that they're selling books.

Some authors have started using their blog as a home page on their websites. The rationale behind this is that the blog is constantly changing and displaying new content. If you have blog software that allows for links, photos, and headers, then the format of the home page could be identical to that of a normal home page. This is your call, and depends on how you want the site to look. If you want lots of room for text and comments, then this might be the way to go.

While you're surfing the Internet for ways to market your book, there's one more way to promote your work. Internet groups have sprung up on every topic imaginable and then some. Most of these on-line "communities" have an electronic list, a method of communication between people with a common interest via e-mails.

Join some of these lists. Don't subscribe to a bunch of lists that you have no interest in, but there are literally thousands of groups out there. Some will hit your fancy. Beyond those groups that are specific to your genre (including MurderMustAdvertise, CrimeThruTime, Cozies, and DorothyL for mystery), there are lists for almost every imaginable interest. Join a few lists that apply to your hobbies, and also join some lists that apply to any topics that are covered in your novel. Join some lists specific to your hometown or your region. These can be especially useful for marketing, and might also give you ideas for future books.

Remember it's not all about you. Be sure to learn the rules of the list. Some do not allow signature lines (those little advertisements just below your name in an email). Others do not allow you to mention your own titles. Some frown on BSP, but encourage discussions of other titles.

Establish yourself now as a member of the list. Don't wait until two days before your book is released to sign up for all the lists. That smacks of opportunism, and people will quickly glom on to the fact that you joined to promote yourself. By subscribing now, you have the opportunity to make a few postings to the list before your book comes out, and then make a general announcement when the book comes out. It's less gratuitous and more people from the lists will be willing to look it up and with any luck, buy a copy.

For the meantime, just join some lists that appeal to you and make posts on whatever the subject is of the list. As of this writing, the majority of the on-line community lists are located at www.yahoogroups.com. Yahoo! Groups allow users to manage their lists and the frequency of their incoming e-mails. I would suggest a daily digest format to keep the e-mails to a manageable minimum. I moderate MurderMustAdvertise, a group that discusses the subject of book marketing and public relations. While my group does not allow self-promotion for its own sake, many members share their ideas with the group and include information on their books as well. So if you share a particularly good use for a business card, you can tell how you used that card in the promotion of your book, Insert Title Here.

Don't stop at the Yahoo! Groups, though. You should do some searches to find if there are any other lists that apply to your interests as well. Many university departments also run e-mail lists for topics that they specialize in, including authors, specific genres and areas of study. Usually, the general public outside of the university community is allowed to join these lists.

You're almost prepared for your marketing venture, but all this is for naught if you don't have a book. You'll need to make sure that the publisher is planning on creating advanced reading copies (also called advanced review copies or ARCs.) These are no-nonsense copies of your book, formatted and printed by the publisher. Typically, they will not have cover art on them, and will not look quite as nice as the finished product. Chances are some of the copy edits haven't been completed, and some of the formatting has not been taken care of. The purpose of the book is to serve as a review copy, and the niceties of printing haven't all been observed.

Usually the publicist for the publisher will take care of mailing the ARCs to the major review sources. If your book is coming out in hardback, you have a good shot at being reviewed by one of the primary publications, *like Publishers Weekly, Kirkus*, the *New York Times Book Review, Library Journal, Library Talk, Booklist*, and others. The publicist should handle this. More than likely, she's built up a retinue of contacts and sources over the years, and has a much better shot at getting the major reviews than you do.

If the publisher sees that you are dedicated to promotion (and hopefully you've started showing this already), they are usually agreeable to giving you copies to send out to local reviewers. On the local scene, presumably you have more contacts and ideas of who to send to. The

ARCs might not look like much, but they run around $10-12 per copy. So there should be no fooling around with them. Only ask for as many as you need, and send back any extras.

If the publisher is unwilling to send you any or doesn't have any extra copies, you should make your own copies for ARC purposes. Make a copy of the printed manuscript, put a cardboard backing and a clear plastic cover on it. Bind the pages in a plastic ringed binder. Be sure to put a sticker on the plastic cover, telling the reader that this is an uncorrected proof, and that it is not for resale. There's a burgeoning market in ARCs these days, as a collecting rarity.

These ARCs should be sent out with a short letter, informing the reviewer of the publication date and the marketing plan for the book. If you're planning a tour of any kind, that information should be related in the letter as well. The book is more likely to be reviewed if the reviewers feel that the publisher believes in it.

Timing is important for the ARCs as well. Most pre-publication reviewers want to see the book three months before the publication date. Sending out books to be reviewed when you get your copies at the time of publication is too late for these sources. That timeframe gives the publication time to assign the book to a reviewer; it gives the reviewer time to read the book and write the review; finally, the publication can schedule the review to appear in the magazine closer to your pub date. Nothing is worse than having a great review too far before publication, and most magazines don't want to be perceived as behind the times by reviewing a book months after publication.

There are sources that don't mind reviewing books after publication, but you'll need to know which are which. There are a number of magazines, newspapers, and on-line sites that review books after publication. You should make use of these sources, because a good review is a very effective method of publicity. Not only will it attract readers, good reviews can be used for multiple purposes. You will want the reviews in your press kit. They should be sent to the distributors so they can see that the book is getting good publicity and should generate more sales. The reviews should be included in your on-line presence via your website. You'll also want to add the reviews to the websites of all the on-line booksellers who are selling your title.

One of the marvels of modern technology has replaced the old-fashioned "clipping service." You can now sign up for a Google Alert, which allows Google to send you any mention of you that is added to the web. Obviously the same issues apply in terms of the slowness of the web spiders, but this is an easy way to find every mention of you that comes along. You'll want to be able to find all of your reviews for the press kit, the distributors, and possibly for future books. Many second or third novels rely on reviews from earlier books instead of going through the entire blurbing process again. The reviews from notable publications carry the same weight as author quotes.

Even though you have two to three months before publication, there are still things to do. Next up you'll be creating a press kit for your work.

Chapter 5
Let's Be Sociable

Social Networking Sites Discussed in This Chapter

Facebook   www.facebook.com
Twitter   www.twitter.com
LinkedIn   www.linkedin.com
GoodReads   www.goodreads.com
LibraryThing   www.librarything.com
Shelfari   www.shelfari.com
Klout   www.klout.com
Oomph   www.oomph.com

One of the latest developments for on-line promotion is social networking. These sites are designed to bring together people with similar interests, and geographical considerations to chat, blog and e-mail. Many of these sites are ideal for introducing authors to readers.

Social media refers to the entire process of web-based and mobile (cell phone) technologies which open a dialogue between two parties. This is a rapidly changing field and what I might tell you today may not be true six months from now and will likely be unrecognizable in two years. Despite the changes in technology and platforms, the concept behind social media will remain the same: talk to the book buyers using the computer.

In today's world, the backbone of social networking is Facebook. In order to get started, you'll need to get a personal Facebook page. There's no way around it. You don't have to put much on it if you choose not to, but you might want to make it presentable for reasons we'll get into shortly.

Presentable in Facebook terms is going to mean:

- A photo of you or a book cover.
- A short biography
- Links to your website, blog, and Twitter webpage
- A bibliography of your works

Of course, other things can be added to the page to make it more interesting and more personal. I've added photos of me in first grade, book covers, photos of some of the authors I've written about and such.

The next thing that you'll want to do is set up lists. Lists are ways to organize and segregate your Facebook friends. On my page, I have a unique list for my family, coworkers, high school friends, college, friends, librarians, writers I know, writers who know me, and readers. The reasons to set up lists are many. You can set up permissions for which lists can see what content. So if you post a photo of your new niece, you'll likely only want that to go to family. If you post big news about your work, you might want to keep that to just the coworkers.

One of the pluses of lists is that you can send mass messages to the people in that list. It's an easy way to communicate quickly with a group of Facebook users. Don't go overboard with this feature. It's easy to get carried away, but only use it to announce new books, nominations, contests and such. No one wants to know your daily word count in an email.

The last category I have is readers. While many authors include readers on their personal Facebook page, other options exist. Since Facebook has a limit to the number of friends you may have on one page (5000), you may wish to consider having an author page. The author page is a separate page where your readers can go, chat with each other, get updates from you, and such. Migrating people from your personal page to your author page can be something of a hard sell. People have become accustomed to the give and take of a personal page and are less thrilled with clicking on the "like" button for an author page rather than the "friend request" button.

Beth Tindall of Cincinnati Media suggests, "When people you don't know ask to be your friend, it's okay to message them that you'll be glad to be friends, but if they're readers, they may enjoy the community at your author page better."

How do you bring people to your author page? Offer them more and different experiences than your personal page. The first thing you can do is offer free books only on your author page. Nothing gets people to sign up faster than free. Of course, those can be either paper books or e-books, depending on what you're promoting at the moment. You can offer live chat options on the page, where you answer questions or discuss books on the page. You can Skype, talk via the computer's audio and video capabilities, and more. I'm in the process of converting old cassette tapes of conferences and presentations into podcasts, which will be offered on my author page.

Author pages are the place to put your photos from conferences, conventions and book signings. You can "tag" or identify the people in the

photograph using Facebook. That will bring th...
to your page to see what the photo looks like.

Erin Mitchell created this chart to compare the...
for Facebook.

Profile https://www.facebook.com/ karinslaughter	Page https://www.facebook.com/ AuthorKarinSlaughter
Personal	Can include personal info, but pages are associated with businesses, brands, organizations, or famous people (think "entities")
Friends	Subscribers (also called Fans or Likes)
5,000 Friend Limit	No Limit
Friends must be approved	No approval process
No analytics	Analytics including demographics and location of your page fans for the page as a whole and specific posts
Only friends can post to profiles (this setting can be changed if you like)	Anyone who is a fan of a page can post to that page
Has pre-set sections (the stuff in the menu on the left) that you can choose to show or hide.	Has both pre-set and broadly customizable sections (sometimes called pages or tabs...just to be confusing). Can add anything you could add to a website.

Be sure to promote your author page on business cards, in your signature lines on emails and other places. That should be the page that you encourage readers to go to. Granted, some readers will locate and

; the author page more exciting
there instead.

: same content to both your per-
meone who belongs to both, it's
ray out and not bothered to come
bvious when you've cut/paste the
her.

uthor Jenny Milchman, "Keep the
of the people you meet will buy your
s might happen right away--or some
ire building relationships, widening
your social w...   reat books, then as a writer you will be
doing everything right."

Before we leave Facebook, let's talk about their ad program. Facebook allows ads on the right hand column of the status feed page and the
individual pages. These ads are seen by everyone on the site. Note that
Google Adwords is much the same and will not be discussed separately.
The programs are very similar, enough so that it would be redundant.

In terms of typical Internet marketing, set the bar very low for
Facebook ads. For whatever reason, Facebook users do not click through
on ads. Marketers have speculated that it may be because Facebook users
are there to connect with others, not buy things, so they choose not to
click-through and leave the site. The typical click-through rate is approximately 0.02-0.04%. In layman's terms, for every 10,000 people who look at
the ad, two to four people will click on it.

Still you shouldn't despair, because the ad sits there the entire time
the user is on Facebook. So they'll see the ad as they read all of the status
messages flowing by in their feed. It's a matter of visibility rather than sales
here.

So how do you establish an ad? You'll need an image, a URL and
a few words of text. Facebook will help you create the ad itself. Then you'll
be asked to set a price for click-throughs. You can set any price you want,
but my experience has shown me that if you go lower than Facebook's
recommended price, you will not get very many views. I tried it, and went
days without any views. Once I set the price to their recommendation, I
had over half a million views the first day.

Not to worry. You don't have to spend your entire budget on these clicks. Facebook allows for a maximum budget, so that you set how
much to spend a day. In testing the program, I set it extremely low, but the
choice is yours.

Obviously with a click-through rate of 0.02-0.04% you will not
break even if you try to make this ad about book sales. There's no way that

can happen. However, much like the QR codes discussed earlier, you can lead your clicks to your fan page, your newsletter sign-up, or a contest or special content just for the users who click-through to your site.

Now that you have your Facebook pages made, you're off to Twitter. Twitter is a website that allows users to post 140 character messages to those who follow them. Your goal should be to get enough users to start making an impact on your sales. John Locke says that it's good to start with 1,000 followers on Twitter.

To the person who has just signed up and has exactly zero followers, that can seem daunting, but it can be easily fixed. I kid you not, I had a dozen followers before I even posted a single message. People are interested in following interesting authors and what they have to say.

To begin, you should start by signing up to follow others on Twitter. The website is very friendly and will help you to find authors to follow and people in your other interests. Follow a number of them (preferably over 100) to start with and you're on your way.

Before we start, there are two characters that you'll need to be aware of. The first of these is the @ sign. In Twitterese, the @ sign comes before a Twitter user name so that you can address the person directly on Twitter. These mentions are good if you're chatting directly with someone or want to mention a particular person by name. (e.g. "@JeffrMarks, I love the new Intent to Sell")

The other character that you need to be aware of is the # sign, which is call a hashtag in Twitter. The hashtag typically precedes a topic. Tweets, what Twitter messages are called, will be included in the topic if the hashtag are used with the topic name.

What are some of the hashtags important to writers? To name just a few:

- #amwriting
- #amediting
- #writer
- #writers
- #writing
- #wordcount
- #wrotetoday
- #publishing
- #wip (work in progress)
- #novels

There are hundreds more out there, but this is just a smattering of the hashtags that you can employ when sending out a Tweet. You can post a few messages to talk about the number of words you wrote today and how the work in progress is coming. People will start to take notice of your Tweets and you'll add followers at a rapid rate.

In addition to the hashtags, some writers want to send their followers to a particular website as part of the message. So if the website that you want to direct people to is over 140 characters or long enough that you can't add a message to it, what do you do? Tiny URL is the place to go. TinyURL.com is a site that converts your website URL or the site of your book or a sales site and converts it into a much smaller URL.

This is the URL for the Kindle edition of my biography, Who Was That Lady?

http://www.amazon.com/gp/product/B00394F3VU/ref=s9_simh_gw_p351_d5_g351_i1?pf_rd_m=ATVPDKIKX0DER&pf_rd_s=center-5&pf_rd_r=1XV7M3RVAZY8PZ30J1N3&pf_rd_t=101&pf_rd_p=470939291&pf_rd_i=507846

Here's the Tiny URL version: http://tinyurl.com/3gy2x4l

Suddenly the URL for my book is small enough that I can post a short message and the URL that I want to send. It takes an additional step, but it's well worth it to post the sales site. Twitter has also added shortening logic to the site, so TinyURL may be a thing of the past. Other people feel that bitly.com is a better site to shorten website URLs as well.

So what do you say on Twitter? If you're shy about getting started, there's a feature called ReTweet. With ReTweet, you are simply passing on a message from someone you follow to your followers. So essentially you're just a conduit of information. This can work well with contests and giveaways. You can supply information for your followers without having to come up with a wonderful quote in 140 characters or less.

And quotes are another way to go. Find a few quotes on a subject and put those out there for your followers as well. Remember they have to be pithy as you are dealing with 140 characters, but it's not difficult to do.

Then synergy can start to take place too. If you want, you can tie your Facebook author page and your Twitter account together. By doing so, all the content you post on your Facebook author page will immediately become Tweets. You'll need to remember that 140 character limit as anything too long will be truncated. I tend to be a wordy so-and-so, and that gets me in trouble at times, but it's an easy way to generate additional content without much work.

You'll need to be mindful of not repeating too much of the content. There's no benefit to following an author if you can read the exact same things on his/her Facebook personal page, author page, or Twitter. It's monotonous and lazy. I am immediately turned off, and usually I do turn off one or more of the avenues of information.

Also do not post your messages from Twitter to your Facebook page. There's nothing I hate more (and I know it's my pet peeve) than getting a status update that's more hashtags and @ signs than text. Be mindful of pushing information in that direction.

Even if I'm retweeting, using quotes, and tweeting the content from my author's page, I should be doing more. There should be specific content for your Twitter followers. One reason is the risk of duplication of messages, as I mentioned before. The other reason is that it becomes easier to see what content and what media is providing you with the most hits on your website and your sales pages. If it's all repeated, I'm only guessing as to what works. By making each one unique, I can see what is working. You don't want to spend hours creating a book contest on Twitter if it doesn't generate any hits. You want to reuse the ideas that generate the most buzz for your book while always looking for other ideas that can add to the mix.

There are third-party software packages that are a bit more user friendly than the Twitter website. One of those is Tweetdeck, which is a separate application that can be used to create Tweets and monitor all of the functions of Twitter. There's also an app for iGoogle that shows you your Twitter feed as well. Many others exist for smartphones, tablets and other portable devices.

Another social networking site is LinkedIn. LinkedIn is a site that uses professions and employers to tie people together. In this manner, it is not as friendly to authors and bookselling as Facebook. I use this site more for contacts and freelance work. It is not design for bookselling or marketing per se, and as a result, I know many authors who created an account on this site, only to let it sit unused.

One thing I have found that you can use LinkedIn for is to increase the number of fans on your Facebook author page and Twitter followers. There are places on LinkedIn where you can request followers for your Twitter account and other places where you can request fans for your author page. Other than that, do not expect to sell many books on LinkedIn.

There are a number of add-ons and tabs that can be added to the author page in Facebook. They are boxes that will show up as part of your newsfeed for the page or they are additional tabs that show up at the top of the page as well. One of these that is easy to use is GoodReads. Good-Reads.com is a site that catalogues your library as well as what you're reading now. You can review books, tell others what you are reading and discuss books in general.

GoodReads also has a wonderful giveaway program. You can run contests from the site and specify how many copies you want to give away and how long you want the contest to run. GoodReads does maintain control of the information of their participants, so you can't add all of these people to your mailing list when you're done, but you can encourage them to go to your site and join. The program is limited to paper books at the moment, but there is some talk of opening it to e-books as well.

They also include a widget that can be shown on your website or other pages that is a click-through to the giveaway as well. This gets the word out to more people about the contest. It's a very easy way to have someone else manage giveaways for you.

Since I write biographies as well, I use GoodReads to tell my readers what particular book by the subject I'm reading now. When I recently wrote my biography of Erle Stanley Gardner, all of my readers could see which book I was reading by Gardner and towards the end, I had a contest where the person who guessed when I would finish all the book won some books by Gardner and by me.

Two more quick applications and we're done. The first is Klout. Klout is a site that determines a score for you based on how well you're handling your social media. Klout provides a dashboard to see if you are driving discussion and influencing people to go to the sites you suggest. This is a good way to see if your marketing is doing what you want. This site just provides a reality check to see if you're doing as well as you'd like with your social media.

If all of this seems overwhelming, there are aggregator sites that will help you manage all the posts and Tweets and links. One of these sites is Oomph, which allows you to schedule Tweets, status updates and the likes. For someone who works long hours at a day job or is planning a vacation or booksigning trip, you can schedule updates before you leave and then not worry that no one is helping to manage your sales. These sites can allow you to work a few hours on a single site and manage all of your social media.

The same caution applies to social networking sites as most of the other on-line activities: keep your time here under control. I use the same photos, same biography, and same interests on all of the sites. I log-in daily to check messages and look at friend requests, and once a week, I add new content (possibly a previously posted blog or new photos) to keep my page near the front of the search engines. They can become time consuming and a distraction. As award-winning author Laura Lippman says, "As a self-employed writer, I love Facebook, which provides the kind of social outlet not available to me. But I also realize that logging a lot of time on the Internet isn't good for me, so I've set pretty strict limits. I don't use the Internet on the weekend (although I check e-mail) and I limit my Facebook time to an hour after my a.m. writing time and another hour later in the day. I also follow a few people on Twitter because my younger friends tend to use it to share about their lives. And when I follow those rules, I feel happier, calmer, saner. Just as one feels better when one eats right. The occasional binge won't wreck anyone, but a steady diet of online life is clearly bad for me."

Chapter 6
The Press Kit

Waiting for publication is difficult. The urge to see your name on the spine of a book and to feel the bound book in your hands can overpower you. While waiting for publication, you need to stay busy. One of the most important things to complete during this time is the press kit.

Many people throw up their hands in despair at the thought of making a press kit, but this little package is one of your most helpful tools in getting interviews and booksignings. Think of the press kit as a business card for your novel. Just in the way that calling cards were used to judge the worth of gentlemen callers a century ago, press kits can wow a potential contact or leave them flat. Which would you rather present: a few snapshots of the author along with a letter or a professional 8"x10" with a separate page for the blurbs, the author's biography, and a press release for the book. You're a professional now, and you have to present an appropriate image to the public.

This packet of information will be your first introduction to many media people and bookstores. So it's in your best interest to have a complete, professional-looking package. Many bookstores will ask for a press kit when you call to request a signing. Additionally, many stores use the information in the press kit to announce your signing in their newsletters and store promotions. Keep in mind that hundreds or thousands of people might be judging your book from the details you put in your press kit. No pressure, right?

Some authors pay to have a PR professional create their press kit, but in all honesty, this is a relatively easy product to develop on your own. No special skills or knowledge are required. Just a bit of creativity and time. The whole process shouldn't take you more than ten hours or so to complete, and as we said before, it will take your mind off the wait until your book becomes a physical reality.

At the very least, a press kit should contain the following:

- Photo
- Book Jacket Cover

- Biography Sheet
- Press Release
- Any Press Mentions
- Five Questions
- List of Likely Questions

The paper press kit needs a folder to hold all the materials. (See the end of the chapter for the electronic press kit.) You shouldn't staple everything together and you can't fold the material to stuff the pages in a regular business size envelope. You'll need a nice thick covered folder to protect your materials from the postal service, and to present them to your audience. The folders you used in junior high school, the colored pocket folders, are perfect for the task. You don't want to buy any of the binders with the three-hole punch prongs along the spine. You won't be punching holes in any of your enclosures. Just the standard two-pocket folder will do nicely.

You have an option at this point —decorate the folder or leave it plain. If used, the decorations should be simple. Perhaps the book cover glued to the front of the folder. Or the name of the book emblazoned in big letters across the front of the folder. Just remember to keep the decorations clean and pertinent to the purpose of the press kit.

Once you have the folder, it's time to start filling it with information about you and the book. The first thing that you'll need is a professional 8"x10" photograph of yourself. Why professional? This photo can appear anywhere, and you want a likeness that is crisp and easy to reproduce. I've seen my face in the newspaper, in programs and flyers, and on poster-sized announcements at the bookstores — the very print that I included in my press kit. You don't want to send the snapshot of you sitting with Aunt Janet. It just won't work to a readership of 10,000.

On the other hand, professional does not mean overly made-up. Stay away from the glamorous shots that are so popular at malls. The soft-focus, the upswept hair, and the rouged cheeks might be fine for your husband's birthday present, but not for your book promotions. Most people can spot these photos a mile away, and they won't fool a soul when you actually come to the store for a signing, looking more like yourself and less like the heroine of a romance novel. The only possible exception to this suggestion would be for romance writers who might want to project an aura of beauty and glamour.

The 8"x10" is a necessity. First, it's the ideal size to fit in the folders that you've purchased. It's also a good size to show the print's definition. Because the photograph can be used for many purposes, it needs to be high-resolution. I've had bookstores create larger than life posters from the photo in promoting the book. A snapshot that's a touch blurry will give an unrecognizable headshot. It's daunting enough to have poster-sized photos of you without them being grainy or indistinct.

This is just a pet peeve of mine, but send a relatively recent photograph of yourself. No one is fooled using a picture that was taken when Jimmy Carter was president. It's not necessary to have a new picture snapped for each book or article that comes out, but try to update your photo every five to seven years. After that, the different fashion trends in clothing and hairstyles start to give away your secret. You don't want to be sitting at a booksigning beneath a photo of you from the disco era wearing a leisure suit, and have potential buyers assume that you're sitting there to rest your feet. Recognition is a key marketing concept, and your appearance is part of that.

The one last thing you'll need to get in relation to the photo is the right to use the photo as needed. In most cases, a professional photographer maintains rights to the photo and the right to reproduce it. Most photographers are happy to release the rights to you for an additional consideration and typically, a photo credit attribution (that's the little line that says "photo by Joe Camera"). Still your agreement needs to be explicit on this matter.

After the photograph of you, perhaps the most requested item from a press kit will be a reproduction of the book jacket art. This will also be carried in newsletters, articles, and for booksigning posters. Depending on your publisher, the timing of the cover art can vary drastically. Some publishers will ask for your input into the cover, and send you drafts (which can be used for promotional purposes). Others will present you with a finished cover shortly before the book comes out. Once you have the cover art, you'll need to make high-quality color reproductions of the cover. Most office supplies stores and copying services will make color copies for about a dollar a page. Put it on glossy paper if the store provides it, and make it on 8.5"x11" paper for the press kit.

If you've been following this book's advice, the next piece of information to be included should be simple. You'll need to include a one-page listing of all the cover quotes you've accumulated for the book. Just title the page with something like "What People are Saying About My Book" and include the quotes that you've received from authors and booksellers. Just as some readers will be drawn to a book by the authors who have provided blurbs, some bookstore and media people will be impressed by the quotes. Try to keep the blurbs to a single page with breaks between each quote for legibility.

The next pieces of information are designed to help the over-worked bookstore people and the media folks. The first page that you'll need is a single page biography sheet. While it's not a necessity to come up with a standard biography that you use in most places, a template bio will save you time in the long run. Most convention program books, media reports, and bookstore newsletters use a short biography as a way of introducing you to their audience. If it's repeated from place to place, people will begin to remember what's being said about you. Even more important, they'll remember what you write.

For example, my standard biography reads as follows,

Jeffrey Marks is a long-time mystery fan and freelancer. After numerous mystery author profiles, he chose to chronicle the short but full life of mystery writer Craig Rice.

That biography (**Who Was That Lady?**) encouraged him to write mystery fiction. **The Ambush of My Name** was the first mystery novel by Marks to be published although he has several mystery short story anthologies on the market. His works include a second Grant novel (**A Good Soldier**), **Atomic Renaissance: Women Mystery Writers of the 1940s/1950s**, and **Criminal Appetites**, an anthology of cooking related mysteries. His latest work is a biography of mystery author and critic Anthony Boucher.

He is the long-time moderator of MurderMustAdvertise, an on-line discussion group dedicated to book marketing and public relations. He is the author of **Intent to Sell: Marketing the Genre Novel**, the only how-to book for promoting genre fiction.

His work has won a number of awards including the Anthony in 2009 and the Barnes and Noble Prize, and he was nominated for a Maxwell award (DWAA), an Edgar (MWA), three Agathas (Malice Domestic), two Macavity awards, and four Anthony awards (Bouchercon). Today, he writes from his home in Cincinnati, which he shares with his dogs.

In ten sentences, I've summed up my writing work and my life. You'll find this biography on my website, several of my book covers, and more program books than I care to count. This is an aid to overworked book people because this biography can pretty much be used verbatim in a press release, an article about my books, or a newsletter from a bookstore. A newspaper is much more likely to run a small piece on you if they can gather the necessary information from the press kit — without picking up the phone to call you.

Of course, the biography page doesn't cover every detail of my life. I don't want it to. I specifically do not mention my day job (which has changed) or relationships. It doesn't mention the articles I've written or my time as a magazine reporter in the insurance field. Your collection of South American butterflies or stamps of Sudan might be fascinating to you, but unless it has to do with the products you're promoting, leave these details out of this biography. If someone calls for a more in-depth interview, mention those interests.

If you look at my sample biography, you'll see that each detail ties back to my writing. With the release of my third biography in 2008, I changed my biography to reflect more non-fiction. I removed much of the information about my mystery series, and focused my attention on the biographies and how-to book I've written.

After the bio, you'll want to give the bookstore people an idea of your writing history. The bottom portion of the bio sheet should reiterate your writing credits and awards. If this is your first published fiction, just list that along with the publisher, price, publication date, and ISBN. Keep the biography sheet to a single page.

You should update the bio sheet after the release of every book or so, but don't change it drastically. For instance, with the release of a second Grant mystery, I left the biography the same until the sentence about my first mystery novel. In this way, readers (who are the people who buy your book) will still recognize most of the biography, even if it's been updated.

Next up is the press release. While the "newsworthy" event is the actual physical publication of your book, put the press release in the press kit to show the media people that you plan on marketing your book. In some cases, authors will include a list of ads, book tours, and other promotions to show the amount of confidence they have in the success of their product

The Internet has a number of templates for creating a standard press release, including Microsoft [http://www.microsoft.com/download/en/search.aspx?q=press+release]. Beyond the specific information necessary to get the book into the hands of the reader, the standard information on the press release will include a date of release, the place of the event (your town), and contact information. This is important so that if the editor or bookseller is interested, they can contact you (or the publisher if you prefer) directly. If privacy is a concern, only include an e-mail address and/or a fax number for points of contact. Both are readily available, and are non-intrusive means of communication.

The press release will be a one-page document announcing the publication of your book. It will have the publisher, price, publication date, and ISBN prominently displayed. If the cover is available, place the graphic at the top of the page. The body of the press release should contain three parts. The first piece of the press release should tell the reader why this announcement is important to them. We all know that it's important to the writer, but specifically why should the reader care about one more book on the shelves of a store? With my Craig Rice biography, I pitched it as the biography of a woman who had once been at the top of the heap, and who had fallen, a riches to rags story. What had happened to one of the top mystery writers of the 1940s? Wouldn't readers want to know that? If you're writing about a new time period for a historical mystery, an area of the country never used before as a background for the detective, or the protagonist with an infirmity of some sort, any of these can be used to tell the reader what is new and different about your book. If the bookseller or reporter gets 30 press releases a day, then what specifically sets yours apart? You should put as much time into crafting the language for the press release as you spent on the query letter to your publisher.

After the lead-in, the next paragraph should be the biography that you created from your biography sheet. I told you that this would come in handy! The biography can be added into the press release verbatim. If it has been written properly, the biography should mesh well with what you've written on why your book is unique. The first paragraph should be a brief synopsis of the book. The biography starts the second paragraph.

Finally, include a few words about your publisher. Back in the day when all the publishers lived in New York, this was not necessary. Everyone knew all the publishers. Not any more. With small publishers, e-books, and such, there are any number of publishers located around the country. Unless your book is coming out from Random House or Putnam, you might want to add a few sentences regarding the publisher. This is a recent development, but one that helps booksellers and reporters to understand how the publisher operates. This is more important to the bookseller who might not be familiar with the publisher even if the major distributors represent the publisher. Additionally, this is the section of the press release to mention a book tour, advertising and other promotional events.

The next two pieces of the press kit are more creative in nature. The first is a mock Question-and-Answer Interview with you playing the roles of both interviewer and interviewee. Come up with a list of about five questions, the type that you hear often from fans: the old stand-by "Where do you get your ideas?", "When did you start writing?", "What are your writing habits?", "What are you working on now?". Then answer those questions to the best of your ability. Don't be afraid to polish them a few times. This is the one item in your press kit that shouldn't be limited to one page. Expound (within reason) about the topics you've selected. Be creative. Be funny. The nice thing is that at this point, you have the time to edit your answers and hone them into a reasonable interview with the author.

The Q&A is useful to reporters and bookstore people. First, it's a ready source of quotes on a variety of topics that they can use without contacting you again. This is convenient for them, and comes in a hard copy format that precludes any misunderstandings or bad quotes. The Q&A also demonstrates that you're articulate enough to carry on a conversation with the media on the most likely topics to be covered in an interview. No reporter wants to have to carry an entire interview with someone who can't compose a full sentence.

The Q&A interview is a good exercise for you as the author as well as a useful tool. The questions force you to start thinking about some of the discussion topics that you'll stumble across as an author. This is your opportunity to come up with stock answers surrounding those topics. You have the time to develop witty, coherent responses. In answering these questions for your press kit, you'll be able to store them away for the next time those queries come up, and they will *repeatedly*. So not only are you adding to your press kit, you're also preparing yourself for the next step in the media process, the live interview.

I was on a live radio interview last year in which we went through the normal interview questions. The last thing the radio host asked was, "If you could invite three people to dinner (living or dead), who would they be?" I was stumped. I'd never thought of this question, and I had no ready answer. Suddenly, I was stumbling for an answer and not sounding very intelligent. I finally came up with three guests, but afterwards I thought of many different people who would have given the listeners a better idea of who I was. Unfortunately, my opportunity had passed.

The last thing that you need in your press kit is the list of likely questions stemming from your book. As I indicated earlier, reporters are overworked. So if you provide them with a list of reasonable questions pertaining to the book, they are more than grateful. Chances are they will not read your book. That's a hard reality to get used to after you've spent years creating your work, but it's the truth. They might look at the cover, read the blurbs, and scan the back cover for a synopsis, but with multiple interviews a day, they simply don't have the time to sit down, read 250 pages, and take sufficient notes on what would make good interview topics. In providing a list of questions, you're helping them out by saying, "Here are the subjects that will make a reasonable interview and are pertinent to the book." Even if they haven't even cracked the spine, no reporter wants to look like they haven't done their job. Before one television interview, the TV anchors came into the green room holding the book and said, "Tell me what this is about." I gave them a synopsis that they repeated verbatim on the air ten minutes later.

The added benefit of the question sheet is that you are establishing most of the questions to be asked during an interview. This means that you should have answers for these questions. You're automatically prepared for the interview.

Once you start calling stores and media, you'll be asked to mail out the press kit. You'll need to have 9"x12" envelopes as well as a cover letter. Even if you create a nice form letter beforehand, take the time to type in the name and address of the recipient. With a computer, this only takes a few seconds to give you a personalized letter. It's worth the effort because media people are more likely to respond to personal messages than to form letters. If they receive a "dear media person," letter, the assumption will be that another media outlet is covering the story and it won't be fresh.

You'll hear of a number of other things that can be included in a press kit. There's nothing wrong with adding more, but they aren't requirements. You might throw in some bookmarks, postcards for the book, or your business cards. Some people want to include posters announcing a signing, but it's a bit premature for that. The store has only asked to see your press kit. You shouldn't send the posters and other material for the signing until the store agrees to have you. Posters are not cheap and it would be a shame to include them in packages that will never result in a signing.

The only other item that can be put into the kit is a copy of reviews of your work. If the publication date is close, you might have some reviews of the book accumulated. If that is so, feel free to include those with the press kit. A review in a publication like *Publishers Weekly*, *Kirkus*, or *The Library Journal* will impress booksellers. Having ready-made reviews of your work is another time-saver to reporters who can use the same review or paraphrase from it.

Once you have the press kit made up, you're ready to start taking your show on the road. So make a few copies of the materials in the press kit, collate them into the folders and pick up the phone to make some calls.

Chapter 7
Finding Your Niche

Humans are social creatures. Even the most solitary of loners still belongs to some groups by virtue of where he lives, what he eats, and what he reads. So what does this sociological fact have to do with book promotions? People are more likely to buy your book if they share something in common with you. Then too, there are groups that will be intrigued by your writing because they are part of a group that is unique to the novel you've written. For instance, if your protagonist is a sewage worker, perhaps a market exists to promote your work to sewage workers across the country.

By identifying yourself as a member of a group, you've identified a niche market for your novel. Look at unique opportunities to market to that audience. Maybe it's as easy as telling a group of fishing buddies that you've published a book, or perhaps the group is so far-reaching that you'll need to consider advertising. Each group is unique and will present distinctive ways of communicating that you'll be able to tap into. For instance, college alumni groups typically have both nationally distributed magazines, and local meeting groups. Your high school alumni group will most likely have neither.

So what groups are you a member of? I'm going to start by listing some of the more common groups. I'm sure you'll find that you belong to one or more. Then you can brainstorm for additional groups of which you're a member. You'll be amazed at how many groups you can come up with in a short period of time.

The first group that most of us belong to is the workforce. I'm not saying that we should define our audience as the entire workforce, but you certainly can slice up your job in a variety of different ways. First, what company do you work for? Most of your co-workers will be interested in hearing about a new book—particularly one written by someone they know. Make a point of telling the people in your office about your new endeavor. There will be some of you who will not be able to talk about your writing. Some bosses will think that your newfound fame as an author will spell the end of your job at work. You'll have to make the call on that. Still, your workplace can be a source of sales.

Don't let timidity stop you from talking about your book at work. In some cases, it's difficult to expound on your own virtues. Working with people tends to be a very goal-oriented situation as opposed to other activities. Even so, mention your interview to them before you're profiled in the paper or on the local radio station. You'll find that some of your co-workers are your best audience. I've always had a great number of people from work show up at my signings.

Beyond the company you work for, you are part of a professional group as well. Currently, I teach middle school English. I belong to the National Education Association as well as the National Council of Teachers of English. While you can't buy mailing lists for all of the professional organizations in your field, there are certainly ways to get your name out there. Submit an announcement of your publication to your professional organization's in-house magazine. Most publications have a column or feature announcing member news. You can tell all of the people in your profession about your book in this manner. Also, be sure to announce the book's release at your local vocational group get-togethers. Bring a copy of your book with you to a meeting, and make a point of showing your book to a few people. If the book is related to your profession, all the better, but even if it's entirely unrelated, be proud of your accomplishment, and tell people where they can pick up a copy of the book.

Now that you've covered your workplace, consider covering your former schools in a similar fashion. Most of you went to high school and college, so you'll have at least two avenues to pursue. Schools, colleges in particular, are ideal places to promote your work. While attending institutions of higher learning, you were in the process of becoming who you are today, which includes your writing. Now that you've accomplished something, they are a great place to tell people about it.

Most alumni organizations have local chapters and a nationally distributed magazine. All of them have a place where alumni can announce their promotions, weddings, and children. Tell the editor about your new book. Local groups usually put out a smaller newsletter for the graduates in the area. Obviously, if you went to school close to where you now live, you'll probably have a bigger population of graduates to whom you can promote your book. With local groups, always try to get a mailing list of the members. Some groups will give or sell you their lists if you're a member.

The national alumni magazines devote pages of copy to the doings of their graduates. Make use of that space to include the details of your book. Submit a photograph along with the article. Find the editor's name and address and pitch a story proposal on your book. If the magazine isn't willing to cover you singularly, try to find a few other graduates who have published and pitch a group article. Most of the magazines are more than willing to do a piece on several alums with a common identity.

Your high school can be another place to sell your book. It's a bit more difficult to get the word out because most high schools are not organized or financially secure enough to send mass-mailings to former students. And typically alumni events are only held every five years, so you could have a book published and out of print in less time than it takes to get around to the next reunion. Still, if an event is coming up that asks graduates what they've been up to, be sure to include your book title.

I've found that speaking to current students at your old high school is a better way of making a strong bond. Most high school English departments these days have a class in creative writing. Offer to teach for a day. The class will be interested to learn that someone who was in their shoes at one time is now a writer. It's good for them, and the talk certainly doesn't hurt the ego — except for the comments about how long ago you graduated.

See if the teacher will allow you to sell books after your lecture. You'd be surprised how much cash the current generation has at their disposal. I do make a point to donate a copy of my book to the school's library and another copy to the teacher. If you're not allowed to sell books to the class, be sure to pass out your signing schedule for the next few weeks after your lecture. Some of them will stop by to say hello, and maybe buy a book.

Having covered the basic organizations, there are numerous other organizations that you belong to, some you might not even be aware of! For example, many mailing lists brokers will sell you a list of the people who live within a short distance of your home. From this list, you can make contact with people the same way local businesses do when they target certain areas or neighborhoods to advertise their services. This can be especially successful if the book is set in your city, since you have a potential audience who shares a home with the author and the book. If you live in an apartment complex or a condominium, post signs about your signings on the public bulletin boards, and ask to have a notice about your book put in the complex's meeting minutes. These minutes are often sent directly to residents.

The number of organizations that you belong to will surprise you. Even your choice of religion can provide you with new marketing opportunities. Your church has a newsletter that can announce your new book. If you fish or hunt or collect glass animals, most of these activities have national organizations that allow announcements as well. Many cozies these days contain a unique hobby or craft that interests the reader. These avocations can be used to market to the relevant craft people; perhaps you can even set up a signing at the local hobby and craft show.

Your family is another source for your work. If your wife works outside the home, she can promote your book to her co-workers. If your husband belongs to the Elks or the Masons, he can tell that group to buy your book. Boy Scouts, Brownies, soccer teams, bowling leagues, PTA, and others are all places where you can find a niche to promote your work.

Tying your book to special interest group by way of themes in the book itself is another way of niche marketing. If you're writing genre fiction, you already have started to promote your work within the genre. We've talked about attending conferences and joining Internet communities related to your genre. All of these things are important. Outside of your immediate locality and your circle of friends and family, the community of readers who are passionate about mystery or romance or science fiction will be your staunchest supporters and the most likely buyers of your books.

Once your book is out, you'll need to make special note of upcoming conferences and events relating to your particular genre's community of readers and writers. You'll want to make your presence known to the attendees. Participate in as many events as your budget allows. If you can't manage to be there, offer a giveaway for a special occasion or auction. Or add postcards or bookmarks to the goodie bags that are passed out at the conference. Be creative in finding ways to make yourself known at a function that you can't attend. Now that your book has come out you'll want to promote it in as many ways as possible. So adding the postcards and flyers to goodie bags can be a good use of time, if done properly. You'll still need to try to find ways that make you and your book stand out from the pack.

You'll also want to be sure that your name is familiar to mystery buyers or romance readers or whichever group your readers are most likely to come from. They'll be more likely to look for your books and pick them up when they are published. There are multitudes of ways to keep your name in front of the die-hard fans. Participate frequently in the online communities. People who never participate are called lurkers and in many cases, people won't even know that a particular author is reading the posts. You don't have to post more than once a week or so, but make sure to comment on a topic being discussed without frequent overt mentions of your books. The signature line of the e-mail will do that for you.

There are a number of genre magazines as well. For the mystery genre, it's *Mystery Scene* or *Deadly Pleasures*. The former periodical has a section of the magazine dedicated to articles where the author tells about the perils of writing this book in their own words. If you write for any of them, you'll get paid for your promotional efforts. If you're not familiar with the magazines that exist for your genre, look them up in an Internet search or consult the people in your on-line community. Most of them are more than willing to answer questions for the novice. If you're not willing to do that, consult a reference guide such as Writer's *Market* to find a list of magazines that cater to a particular genre.

Once you've located the markets, pick up a copy or two of the magazines aimed at the markets you wish to reach. Not only should you read the magazines to find out what the gossip and happenings are of current interest in your field, but you'll also find out about the ads and advertising efforts of other authors. All of this will allow you to investigate the standards of the industry, which you may decide to play to or flout. Look particularly at the columns. Is there a way for you to contact the columnist via e-mail or regular mail? If so, study what the column is about and slant a tidbit about yourself to the columnist. Most of them will be grateful for not having to scrounge for copy for next month. Just be sure that the item fits the theme of the column. You don't want to submit something on your signing schedule to the columnist who is in charge of writing about announcements of new books.

Also check out the magazine's feature articles. Some magazines want articles about "how I did it." Obviously you have one of those stories. Everyone does. The article can help to sell your books if the audience understands where your idea came from and how it came to be a novel. Many people are going to ask you where you get your ideas, anyway. This is your chance to formulate an answer on the topic.

Other magazines prefer to educate readers on a particular subject. By researching a particular topic in the genre, you become something of an expert on the subject and use that knowledge to indirectly promote yourself. In writing the biography of Craig Rice, I obviously learned a lot about her. Yet, I still discovered a great deal about a number of other authors of the era. I've used some of that information to write articles and postings on those authors for mystery readers. Without directly promoting myself, I'm establishing myself as an authority in the field, and that position helps me to sell books.

The final feature that occurs in most magazines in the fiction field is the interview piece. Look at the issues you bought and find out who is responsible for writing the interviews. Is that the job of the editor or do they leave that task to freelance authors? If it's a non-staff writer, encourage a friend or colleague to write an interview with you. That colleague can then submit the article for publication.

On the other hand, if the interviewer is a staff writer, you'll have to pitch the story to that person or the proper editor in hopes of getting in the magazine. In most cases, you'll just need to write to the magazine, and volunteer yourself as an interview subject. You'll need to explain why you're interesting enough for three or four pages of text in the magazine. It's not enough that you've just published a book; all the authors in the magazine have done that. You'll need to have a unique experience or a different method for writing or a singular outlook that sets you apart from all the other writers. That's what the editor wants to hear about: why you'll be interesting enough to make readers want to pick up the magazine.

Outside of the genre functions and publications, there are still wealth of niches to mine in publicizing your book. Hopefully, you have more than just a murder or an alien in your novel. In the same way that you have an environment that can be mined for opportunities, your book has its own world that can be used in a similar fashion. As Carole Nelson Douglas points out, "some authors' books have subject elements that interest specific audiences they can cultivate. In mystery some of these are cats, gardening, food, etc. Authors should look for ways to get the word about their book/ books to publications and conferences that specialize in these interests. It's called niche marketing. You may need to write non-fiction articles for the magazines, or just make sure someone at the publication has a copy of your book for review purposes. Look for a nonfiction angle or "hook" in your fiction books; media always responds better to the "issue" part than to the "story" part of a novel."

For example, my first two mystery anthologies were canine-related. Easy enough to see that they were mystery related, but equally obvious to see the dog tie-in. I took a look at the four-legged market. One of the most prestigious awards in the dog-writing genre was the Maxwell award. So I nominated several of the stories from *Canine Crimes* for the awards and my short story was one of the three finalists. Suddenly all the dog writers had heard of *Canine Crimes*. The nomination was great publicity for the book and allowed me to expand my audience by reaching dog lovers.

Likewise, Carole Nelson Douglas set up a number of book events at Society for the Prevention of Cruelty to Animals (SPCA) locations across the country to promote her Midnight Louie series. The events not only sell books, but the proceeds benefit a worthy cause. Of course, the SPCA advertises the events to their audience, who consists of mostly pet lovers. A great match all the way around.

Dirk Wyle wrote *Pharmacology is Murder*, a hard-boiled mystery with intricate scientific details. When he was looking for places to sell his book, he targeted pharmacologists and toxicologists. Since the book is set in a medical school in Miami, Florida, he marketed to both medical students and people who live in or are familiar with Miami. Additionally, the protagonist belongs to Mensa and lives on a boat, so he promoted his book to both of those groups as well.

Another example is that I've tied books in my Grant series with the recent craze of Civil War reenactors. Almost every city has their own group of reenactors, and this group visits the major battlefields of the war frequently. So I had a built-in audience once I located the Civil War reenactors in my area. I've done a number of events that cater to this crowd, even going as far as having someone come in dressed up like General Grant himself. The group is interested in hearing about how I conduct my research, how I come up with ideas for the series and how I resolve issues where there is disagreement about what really happened in a battle. Their interests overlap with my writing, and in these events I have a very high rate of purchase by the members.

Besides the background and issues of the book, the profession of the main character can be a good way to market the book. With the police detective or the private eye, this isn't much of an option. While some professionals enjoy a good mystery, for most it's like coming home to more work. So you probably won't get a huge following of cops for your hard-boiled books.

But in the case of an amateur sleuth, the profession of the detective can be a drawing point as well. Diane Mott Davidson has catering and cooking featured in her novels. You'll find a wealth of librarians, book collectors, chefs, and gardeners in other books. If you can think of the profession, it's likely that it's been written about. By using a unique profession to gain notice for your book, you'll find yourself getting coverage that is not based solely on the genre; nor will your novel be relegated to just the book pages of newspapers and magazine. If you're only covered in the literary section of a magazine or newspaper, you'll only attract the attention of people who like books. If you're in the lifestyle section or the finance section of the newspaper, you're getting exposure to the people who would not otherwise have read about your book. Julie Wray Herman used her connections to get coverage in the gardening section of the newspaper for her mysteries that feature a landscaping business. The feature highlighted her works and her own gardens. Now horticulturists know about her series of books. One of the best ways to reach a wider audience is through the various subject matters present in your book.

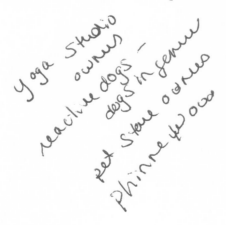

Chapter 8
Us versus Them

Most of the tasks that you're doing to promote your book are considered public relations work. There's a whole field of business dedicated to PR, and of course, a whole field of PR professionals willing to take your dollars to do the job. The publicists at the publishing houses are considered PR professionals. Many authors, especially the more reticent ones, are tempted to hire someone to do the PR work for them. The rationale is that a PR professional saves them time so they can focus on writing another book while the PR person handles all the details of your tour.

So what would you look for in a PR professional? What are the skills and qualifications that you'd want in someone who is handling your career? You want someone who has a proven track record with authors and the publishing industry. It isn't very helpful to find a PR person with a track record in music or theater. You'd still have to explain the concepts of ARCs, ISBNs, distributors, and many other things that you'll find in this book. The more time that you spend explaining these concepts, the less productive the PR person will be. And of course, you'll be charged for the time of their learning curve.

The PR person should have proper credentials. Anyone can hang a sign out announcing a PR firm. After all, my degree is in computers, but I've worked in marketing and PR for a number of years. While I would consider myself something of a marketing pro (as does my publisher since I'm writing this book), I have only a few college credits of formal training in the area. Most of the experience I possess has been learned on the job, either from employers or working with my own books. Still I've done significant media campaigns and worked with most of the major market media.

So how can you find out if the person you're looking to hire has the appropriate credentials to handle your job? Is she a member of Public Relations Society of America (PRSA)? Did he win an award from American Marketing Association? By participating in PR organizations, the handler shows dedication to his field and a willingness to learn more about the profession.

Questions to Ask a PR Professional Before Hiring

- How many years of experience do you have in PR and marketing? (Preferably more than 10 years.)

- What is your background information, your current client load, and what sort of skills and experience does your staff have?

- What is your track record of placements and promotions?

- What authors and publishing houses have you worked for?

- What is the total number of books you have promoted?

- What is your most successful book campaign?

- How many of your clients have been promoted on the national level?

- Can I see a client list?

- Can I see examples of press kits you have created?

- Will I be working with you as my main publicist or one of your staff members?

Ask for references from author clients. A good PR person will have a list of authors who have received national media attention over significant tours. Be sure to look at their list of clients, and choose three or four distinct clients. One good campaign might be a fluke. Three or four should indicate a pattern that the person can deliver the appropriate goods. The three or four clients you choose are the ones you'll want to follow up with in depth. Study the reviews they received, their media spots, and any interview pieces. After doing this, you'll be better able to judge the quality of the PR professional's work. Be forewarned. PR professionals are not cheap. If most authors spend a large sum of money on promotions, I'll bet that they've hired a PR person to help them out. Author Peter Lance spent nearly $30,000 on publicity, a part of which was budgeted for a person to promote his first novel. Unless you have the funds to do this without relying on royalties, be careful about spending this kind of cash on promotions. It could be several books or an entire career before you recoup the money you spend. Lance's contract for his first three books only gave him an $8,000 advance. It takes a lot of novels to pay back that sum.

So what do you pay for when hiring a PR professional? Mostly you're paying for their contacts and writing ability. Part of a PR person's job is to maintain good working relationships with the media and the people who can get you the attention of the media. But guess what? You're well on your way to having your own contacts database, and if you have a book coming out, you obviously have the ability to put words on paper. So there's no reason why you can't do some of this work yourself.

As I mentioned before, some people despise the work of promoting themselves. Even if you hire someone to set up the appointments and the interviews, you're still required to talk. You've only greased the wheel. The time will still come for you to talk to the media, and handle those tough interviews. It's not difficult to schedule your own publicity but you'll need a certain mindset to sell yourself properly. And self-promotion does take a certain amount of time and effort. Most authors that I talk to split their time between writing and marketing. That means spending between ten and twenty hours a week on promoting your own work. Sometimes that can be overwhelming, especially when going on tour, or promoting a just-released title. According to Joan Hess, the author of the Maggody series, during the early part of her career, she would spend up to a quarter of her time engaged in marketing work. As her publishers saw that she was dedicated to her career as a writer, they decided to help. She estimates that she only spends about five percent of her time any more engaged in public relations work.

So what can you expect to pay for a PR person? Here's a chart of some rates for professionals and what you should expect to get from them.

Activity	Low Price	Middle of the Road	High End Price
Press Release and Review	$300	$400	$600
Press Release and bio	$250	$300	$500
Custom Presentation Folders	$2,000	$2,800	$3,500
Custom Envelopes	$250	$500	$750
Blast Fax or E-mail distribution (See page 82)	$500	$700	$1000
Media Campaign	$10,000	$20,000	$40,000

Even individual services can be expensive. Photos can be reproduced, but the fee for that is several dollars per photo, the same price that most of the photography studios charge. By going to the local photo developer, reproductions will cost hundreds of dollars less. Some pharmacies now charge less than 20 cents a print. If you have the image scanned, your computer can print photos for just the cost of the photo paper at the local office supply store.

PR professionals can do most any service associated with good marketing. They can develop advertisements, oversee the best placement of the ads in magazines, and suggest resizing and cuts for the ads. They arrange media events; give you pointers on what to wear and how to speak for each of the different media. That training can include books, audiotapes, and videos about how to talk during an interview. They will also tape a practice interview with you, allowing you to get the feel for the process. It's all very helpful, but you have to remember that they charge by the hour for this service.

Additionally, most PR firms will not guarantee media coverage for you. It's next to impossible to guarantee. If you happen to release your book the same week as a major international skirmish or national election results, no PR person can pre-empt that to get you on the air. The best services will suggest an average of one or two interviews per stop on the tour. Even so, there's no promise that your big interview won't be the community press or that low-wattage local radio station. Some smaller firms, like Breakthrough Promotions, charge by the events they schedule. This can be a significant savings for authors on a strict budget.

A PR professional can set up book signings, develop bookmarks and postcards, design and host your website, develop posters and more. Beyond the staff members who excel at working the media, a typical firm will have a staff of graphic designers who make all the advertising, and a staff of copywriters to create content promoting you and your work. Since the specialization is so delineated, the overhead costs that you'll pay for will increase the price of any project.

One PR company I know of offered to design and host an author's website for $8,500. Even if you consider that two years of reserving space on a web-server could run you $500, you've just agreed to pay over $8000 for the HTML pages they will design for you. Some of the firms even put a 500-megabyte limit on your space on the server. For $8,000, you can buy your own server!

Cincinnati Media created my website, and the websites for Mystery Writers of America and several other well-known authors. The company's prices are competitive with the market and significantly less than what a public relations and marketing firm would charge. Of course, that doesn't include the cost of purchasing the rights to the URL that you'll want. That's extra. Are you starting to get the picture that there are better ways to spend your hard earned and not-yet-earned royalty money?

As you can see, you will pay a great deal of money to a PR professional to do some of the same things that I've been telling you to do. You have to consider if you want to pay someone a truckload of cash to place phone calls for you and fax press releases. Most people don't have that kind of dough lying around. And when you're done doing these things for yourself, you'll retain the resource material. You'll be able to recycle the contacts when the time comes to publish your next book. You'll know the media people, you'll have met the bookstore owners, and you'll have developed the relationships with the reviewers. When a professional does this, he keeps the contacts and takes his marbles with him when he leaves.

If you do opt to hire a PR person, the best use of his time is to get him to help you with the strategic marketing plan. Leave the faxes and the press releases alone, but pick his brain for the ideas and suggestions that he's learned over the years. Get his help with preparing a reasonable budget for your promotions. Have him draw up a schedule of events that need to happen. Have him tell you what techniques have the best return on your investment. Most PR people would be happy to help develop a strategic marketing plan with you.

But what if you're petrified of doing the cold calls and the sales necessary to make a name for yourself? There are other ways to get help that don't involve spending your entire advance. One of the best ways to get assistance is to ask your local university. Find out if the school has a communications program or offers a marketing degree. If they do, contact the individual school departments to learn if they sponsor internships. Most intern programs allow students to work for a particular company (in this case, your writing business) in exchange for college credits. There are a set number of hours required per week for the student to work. In exchange, you pay a small stipend to the school for administrative expenses. You'll give assignments to the intern who can do the job from your house or their dorm room. Depending on the school's academic calendar, you'll get their services for either 10 or 15 weeks.

Of course having an intern means that you'll have to train someone new every term, but the intern approach is thousands of dollars cheaper than hiring a professional. Most of the tasks involved with selling books are more time-consuming than rocket science. The same types of activities are done in any office across America. If you need someone to mail press kits or phone bookstores, you certainly can expect a college student to do that without much training.

Of course, this plan does require some organization on your part. You can't wake up in the morning and decide what you'll be doing to market your book today. You'll have to come up with a master strategy of what tactics to take with the media and bookstores. You'll need to come up with things for the intern to do. You'll be surprised how much work can be fit into 10 or 15 hours a week. That's a lot of e-mails and phone calls. Chances are that if you're months away from publication or six months have passed since the release of your book, you might not have enough work to keep the intern busy.

Typically, the intern can be expected to call media contacts in your city. Local and genre-related bookstores can be notified of your new title. Media kits can be sent out to any interested reviewers or bookstores. The intern can also be responsible for sending out copies of the book to bookstores that request them. Most media people require some sort of press release for their work. If you plan a mass mailing of press releases for the book, the intern can use your contact database to create mailing labels, address the releases and stamp them. All these kinds of things are well within what you could expect an intern to do for you as part of the "course work".

Still, you need to interview the person and see if the student would be responsible and courteous as your representative to the public. Nothing would be worse than having an intern insult people or not follow through with promised events. You want to make sure that the intern will be representing you well in your chosen field.

According to Patricia Wynn, the author of *The Birth of Blue Satan*, she has found some of the best interns outside the business marketing fields. "The students who have been most interested are the ones who have been pursuing other careers, who would like to explore the publishing industry. They are hoping to learn the ins and outs of the business so they can apply that knowledge to deciding what part they might want to play in the industry. They have a variety of skills from their former pursuits, including some web design and database use. All of them are book lovers. They are more likely to understand and support what they are selling than someone with business skills who doesn't have a love for books."

If you can't find someone who will intern for you, hiring a part-time employee is another option for you. Not a PR professional, but an assistant who can do small amounts of work for you. You might pay just over minimum wage to find someone to take care of the clerical work for you. That reduces the time you spend on marketing. It's still significantly cheaper than hiring a PR firm.

You'll have better luck hiring someone you know. You can also advertise in the local newspaper or hire someone from an employment agency. Make sure that you specify that this is a part-time position with no benefits. Interview the person like you would for any other job, asking for skills, desired hours, and references. Definitely take pains to check out the background of the person in the same way you would an intern. This person will be the "face" you present to the public in many arenas, and you want him or her to make the impression you leave on people a good one. Nothing can be more damaging than having a person who is difficult or insulting represent you.

The downside to this approach is that suddenly you're an employer. You'll need to file the appropriate W2s and other tax forms. You'll be responsible for things like unemployment insurance if the person works more than a certain number of hours. All of this is added to the workload of marketing your book. Unless you find truly good help, you might end up doing more work with an employee than without one.

Of course, helpful people are out there who will do things for you at no cost. Family members, friends, and neighbors might be persuaded to help you out around the time of your book launch when the workload is most intense. With this approach, you're not hampered by the tax laws and employment requirements, but at the same time, you're also limited to who is available. You're not likely to get a chance to interview several candidates for the position. If you find a person who offers to work with you for free, take them.

If you have a person who is working for nothing, you will probably want to limit their contact with the outside world on your behalf. You'll have plenty of tasks to keep them busy, but since the person is likely to be related to you, you might want to consider how that would appear to a bookstore or television station. "Hi, this is Shakespeare's mother, and I'm so proud of him. He just wrote this play, and I think you need to read it." The impact is significantly less than if you have an unrelated party calling.

An additional option is to suggest a working arrangement with someone from a local writing group, especially if that author is in the early stages of publishing his or her own book. If Jane is a year behind you in the publication process, letting her help make contacts with the press will give her an idea of what to expect when her book comes out. Plus you're helping Jane by showing her the ropes. She'll get to interact with bookstore managers, and she'll learn how to develop press kits and other important marketing documents. All of this is great experience for her, and help for you.

Of course, if none of these options work, doing the work yourself is always the last and sometimes best solution. You'll have to sacrifice some time from another area of your life to do this, but at least it's only a temporary inconvenience. Things don't really gear up until the weeks just before publication. Most promotional campaigns should be over within about three months of the book's true release date, which means that life can get back to normal. Once the book is readily available, you'll only have a limited amount of time to gather the maximum amount of publicity.

Direct control of your promotions has some benefits. A lot of people are thrilled to talk directly to the author. A benefit of doing the work yourself is that typically you'll know the answers to all the questions booksellers, readers or the media might pose. While an intern might have to check with you and get back to the bookstore, you have all the information at your fingertips.

Just because you're in the midst of promotion doesn't mean that you want to neglect your writing. Promotion is a means of drawing attention to your writing, which should be your primary concern. As indicated earlier, many authors spend a part of each day or set aside days to work solely on their marketing. If you want to keep up in the publishing business, you'll need to keep producing high-quality works to appear in print. Normally, publishers expect you to complete approximately one book per year. That means that you have to continue writing—and writing at a decent pace—to make this quota.

Chapter 9
Judgment Day

There's a certain expectation level surrounding the big day, but the amusing thing about the publishing world is that the publication day is not a firm date set in stone, like your signings. It's more of a suggestion. I've had books that were ready for bookstores weeks before the publication date, and other books that weren't ready until nearly a month after the publication date. Except for the bestsellers, the vagaries of printing make it nearly impossible to pinpoint the day of the actual completion of the process.

So all the preparations should be ready, but in wait mode until the book is on the shelves. You don't want to start putting out promotional material and getting good press if the book can't be found at any bookstores. Distribution problems will waste the best part of the publicity you'll be receiving. Usually I put a few weeks of lag time between the "official" publication date and the ramp up of the promotional efforts.

One of the first signs that tell me that the book is ready to be promoted is the release of the book from the on-line bookstores. On-line bookselling sites put out a notice when the books have been shipped. That's your cue. When you get those notifications that the book is being shipped, you may assume that the book is being properly distributed and you can begin to make those plans to promote your book to the limit.

One of the first things that you'll want to do is issue your press release. If you've created a good press kit, you will already have a press release. So this important document should be ready to go when the book finally hits the shelves. Almost all media people prefer to get press releases rather than phone calls. All the information is included on one page along with quotes that allow for easy conversion to a short article about the book.

You'll be using the database or spreadsheet of contacts that you've been accumulating for this task. This is the phase of your promotional work where you begin to use the items that I've recommended you create in the past few chapters. In addition to the names and addresses of contacts, you should have collected phone numbers, fax numbers, and e-mail addresses. This information will give you some low-cost ways to contact the people who need to know that your book is being released.

If you don't have very many names on your list, there are companies that sell mailing lists. They will provide you with a list of several hundred contacts in a given field for typically less than $100. These companies accept credit card transactions over the Internet, and you can have a downloaded file in a matter of minutes.

Ideally, you'll have your own "in-house" list, the list compiled by you for your purposes. This, of course, is the most accurate and best list for promoting your work. If you must purchase a list, you'll have to know the proper type of list to purchase. Association lists are those that are related to a specific niche group. These are more focused and can be used to market to a particular audience. Response lists are mailing lists where the addressee has answered a previous direct mail request. This means that they are more involved with their mail and could be persuaded to purchase something based on advertising. Compiled lists are the broadest, and are typically just lists based on a particular set of demographics. Since women represent the majority of readers, you can start to narrow your lists based on what you know about your audience. Most companies will allow you to select the criteria for your mailing list. Ideally, you'd want to purchase the names of people who shop on Amazon.com and BN.com and spend over $1000 a year on books from those sites. Most companies will not allow you to be that specific, but the idea is to pick people who are most likely to respond positively to your request. It would be a waste of time and money to market your book to the rural poor in China, when your book is in English.

I've seen lists that cover public libraries, university libraries, book reviewers, industry specific magazines, and many more. If you haven't had much luck in collecting local contacts or if you plan on doing some national touring, you might want to consider enhancing your list with these paid lists. The lists come with guarantees that the data is up-to-date, and the company providing the list will reimburse you if the promotional items are returned to you because of bad addresses.

P.J. Nunn, the owner of BreakThrough Promotions has this to say about press releases. "Probably the best way for authors to distribute press releases is to do so one at a time to specific markets. There's often a temptation to do a multi-market fax or email blitz, and there's not really anything wrong with that if they're going to directed markets. But it's sometimes costly and rarely effective. If the press release is a simple book release notice, then sending to a list of markets via fax or email is good. If the goal is to advertise an upcoming event, or to seek a book review or article opportunity, that's a different story. Search for the most appropriate markets, verify contact information and preferred method of receiving press releases, then customize the release to fit those specs. Once the release has been sent, be sure to follow up by phone in a day or two."

There are three ways to distribute your press release. For the sake of your wallet, I'll cover these in progression from cheapest to most expensive. The first method is e-mail. In looking at your contact list, if the entry has an e-mail address, send the press release to the person's e-mail account. E-mail is a very non-intrusive way of contacting people, and most e-mail programs give you the choice of tagging e-mails with a receipt notice so that you can see if they were received without bugging the recipient.

Most of the major media outlets have supplied their staffs with e-mail, so this should be an easy way to distribute your news. Your press release was probably created in Microsoft Word or a word-processing program that is compatible with that application. In this case, you'll be glad that one piece of software is pervasive. If you have it available, convert the file to an Adobe Acrobat file (PDF.) These files are universally read and typically recognized as not being able to contain a virus or worm. So send the press release as an attached file to the media. If you have any doubts that the people you're sending it to have appropriate software, imbed the press release in the body of the e-mail. This will make the e-mail a larger message, but you'll know that the message was legible to all the recipients.

You might want to consider just including the press release in the body of the e-mail or as a note on Facebook. With so many viruses and worms being spread through e-mail systems recently, a number of potential buyers might just deleted the message without reading it. It's imperative to have a well-defined subject line and an equally well-crafted message in order to allay the reader's fears. If you can live without the colored fonts, bolded lettering, and italicized words, you might just put a plain text version in the body of the e-mail to increase your chances of being opened and read.

You can also create a note in Facebook, which is simply a text document which others can read, based on permissions. If you load your press release to Facebook, you can tag friends in the note to ensure they take notice, or publish something to your wall which announces that you have a new note on your page. Both will guarantee some reads by your Facebook friends.

One way to send the press release out to a wide distribution with a single e-mail is the blind copy. In that way, the recipients won't see the addresses of everyone you are sending the e-mail to. The recipient will only see her name in the "send to" box of the e-mail. Using blind copy for your e-mail avoids giving the impression that you're blanketing the country with your press release, and it also keeps your media list private. However, if possible, it is better to individualize your pitch to the contact through a personal e-mail. If that is not feasible, use less than 35 e-mail address at a time to reduce the chances of being considered spam by many filters.

If your messages are returned, take a look at the e-mail addresses that didn't work. If it's just a matter of poor typing, resend the notes to the media. If it's your contact list, then you'll need to make the necessary changes to your database so that the addresses will be correct next time. The contacts list should be constantly refined and updated. You don't want to waste an opportunity by having the wrong data.

For people on your list who don't have an e-mail address (or more likely in this day and age, you just don't have their e-mail address), fax copies of the press release. Again this is a fairly non-invasive way of contacting the people on your list.

If you only have a few people to contact via fax, fax the releases individually by hand. However, if you have several hundred faxes to send out, consider the use of a broadcast or blast fax. The blast fax software allows you to submit the press release and a list of fax numbers. In most cases, the browser-based client software doesn't take up much of your PC's hard-drive and is free as long as you pay for sending out the faxes via the particular service.

Blast fax software sends the data to a server at its fax service. The fax is attempted until it is properly sent to every fax number you submit or the maximum number of retries for each fax number is reached. You'll get reports back from the service telling you what faxes worked, and what didn't. If the service failed to reach certain numbers after repeated attempts, retry the unsent faxes manually. If you run into errors, update your database with correct information. This might cause you some additional effort, but in the case of blast faxes, it's more than just a bother to have incorrect fax numbers. The fax services charge from $.03 to about $.35 per fax, so if you keep retrying a bad fax number you'll be charged for the incorrect fax numbers as well.

The most expensive, but most traditional, way to send out press releases is by the U.S. Post Office. The press release can be copied or printed as needed, and mailed to the various news agencies. In most cases, you'll want to make black and white copies of the press release, so you might want to remove the cover art graphic from the release. Many authors create a second press release, solely in black and white in order to maximize the clarity without copying a color photo. The time and money to make color copies of the press release could be prohibitive.

Turning once more to the contacts database that you've created, you'll find that most software allows you to generate mailing labels from your contact list. You can use those labels to mail the press releases. Additionally, most word processing programs have a mailing label feature. Just show the application how you want the labels formatted and on what type of label, and the program will create a file of ready-to-print labels. Some programs will even add the bar-coded zip code on the label for easier sorting at the Post Office (and that can reduce the cost of your mailings.)

When sending the press releases, the easiest way to send them is to tri-fold the release, staple it, and then apply the label. A more time-consuming method is to put the labels on envelopes and stuff the envelopes with the release. This is often a better idea if you're worried about the release being mangled in transit. Use regular #10 business envelopes. The 10"x12" size envelopes are unwieldy and are typically more expensive to mail than their smaller counterparts.

There are alternative ways to announce your book's debut. Once the press releases have all been sent out, then you need to make some follow-up calls to the media to see if they got the release, and if they are interested in conducting an interview with you. By keeping your name in front of the media, you're more likely to be asked to do an interview sometime around your pub date.

Another way to bring attention to the book's release is to host a book launch party. There are a number of ways to handle this matter. In years gone by, publishers would host a party for an author's new release and invite the media to the party so they could meet the author in person for possible interviews, as well as make the society page. Have the party as soon as the book comes out; with the provision that you are assured that copies of the book will be available for the party. Usually, book launch parties are held within the first month after release of the new book.

Today with the emphasis on containing costs in the publishing industry, this is a tradition that only survives for the bigger name authors. However, you can still have a party even with fewer attendees and less media attention. Like bridal showers, technically the guest of honor shouldn't host her own party, but the launch can be done on a small budget while still making for a nice party.

The first thing you'll need is a venue for the party. Many people opt to have the party at a local bookstore. One of the nice things about these parties is the ability to sell copies of your book directly to the public. A good bookseller can help you out by having the event at their store, typically after hours, and by carrying a good number of copies of the book. Copies of any reviews the book has received as well as any promotional items that might go over well can be put out for the media people. If you can't find a bookstore that will stay open late for your revelry, rent a private space, or host the party in your home or someone else's home. Still invite a local bookseller to handle book sales. You'll be busy talking to everyone at the party and won't want to deal with the hassle of counting out change.

Besides copies of your book, no party is complete without food and drinks. Don't make people feel that you only want the cover price of your book from them. It is strategically a good idea to place the bookseller near the food, so that people will see the books when they get a bite to eat.

Perhaps, too, you could have background music, though nothing too overpowering. You want to be able to talk to people without shouting. Overall, you want the food and music to complement your book launch party. For a successful party, you'll want to invite friends and family as well as the media. While the party should be geared primarily to the media, invite any number of people to the party. The local media doesn't keep up on sales and book shipments like you do, so they will tend to judge the party by the factors they can see. If the room is jammed with people, they will have to assume that the party is a hit, because the book is a hit as well. It's been my experience that most media people will show up, look around to see if there are any people there (to judge the popularity of the book), and then leave.

Therefore, if you just invite media people to your launch party, you might want to install a revolving door to ensure they have an easy departure. One more thing about inviting media to your launch party, and this is really important to remember: even though the bookseller is selling books to the party guests, never make media members buy their own copies of the book. That's bad form. You should pay for all the copies for the media, just as you would have if you'd received the request via e-mail. You shouldn't make a big deal of the presentation of copies to them. Act like you deal with the media all the time. Keep it low-key, and try not to do it in front of the friends and family who will have to pay for their copies of the book.

One question that will be sure to come up during the process of arranging events around the publication of your book is the question of your book's wholesale distributors. The two most well known wholesalers of books in the U.S. are Ingram and Baker and Taylor. The industry is in a state of flux at the moment, but these two distributors are most well known and used by the majority of the bookstores across the country. Most stores tend to favor one distributor or the other, but you'll find that the majority use one of them. A number of other wholesalers exist. Perseus Distribution Services, IPG, BooksWest, Partners, and others also perform the same function for booksellers.

Wholesalers buy directly from the publishers (usually at a discount of about 55 percent), and then take orders from the bookstores; the bookstores in turn are shipped books at roughly a 40 percent discount. In most cases, larger publishing houses get their books automatically listed in the distributor's computer system. With the smaller houses, distribution of titles by one of the wholesalers can be more of a trial. In order to improve the chances of your book being picked up by a large distributor, smaller publishers should send a listing of the title, publication date, price, and ISBN of your book directly to the distributor. In some cases, the distributor will ask to see a copy of the book. Currently, the major distributors are having a difficult time trying to decide how to handle print-on-demand and self-published titles. While this will eventually get straightened out, you should expect that smaller publishers will have difficulties with larger distributors in the interim.

When you talk with the bookstores about your book, they will ask you if your novel is listed in the computer systems of any of the large distributors. Having your book listed with one of the wholesalers shows bookstores that the company or companies distributing your book believe that there will be demand for your work. Before talking with bookstores, you'll need to ask your publisher what wholesalers are being used to distribute your book. While most bookstores can handle ordering books directly from the publisher, it's much less hassle in terms of invoice paperwork to get all their books from one source. The bottom line: the easier it is for bookstores to order your book, the more likely it is that they'll keep it in stock. Make sure that bookstores know who is distributing your book. While you can assume that your book will be listed with one or more of the wholesalers, it's highly recommended to bring some copies of your book with you to signings. It's nice to think that the bookstore will sell out of your title, allowing you save the day with your extra copies, but in some cases, the store might not have been able to get the book in stock for your signing. Most orders from the distributor will take two to three days to arrive, so timing really shouldn't be an issue, but if the nearest warehouse is out of copies, more time might be needed. If the store didn't plan ahead, this could be a problem.

There's also an on-line site that allows you to view sales of your title. Nielson Bookscan, which was once prohibitively expensive, has now become available for most authors. Many author organizations have purchased a license for Bookscan and allow authors to use it for a fee; additionally, Amazon has set up a service to allow authors to use Bookscan via its website. Bookscan does not cover all stores or sales, but is estimated to cover approximately 60-75% of the market.

The best chance to snag an interview with the media is the time surrounding the release of your book. Reporters want a story that is new and fresh. That only applies to a new release, not a book that's been out for six months. So you'll need to move fast after the release to get those interviews. Just like with the signing, make sure that the book is in the distributor's system, and available through at least one local store before hitting the media hard. Otherwise, you're just wasting the publicity you'll be getting.

Start with the people to whom you sent mailings to. They should at least have a passing knowledge of you by this point. You've sent them a copy of the press release and an invitation to your book launch party, so your name should be familiar to them now. It's extremely difficult to catch a media person on the phone. Chances are that you'll get their voice mail or an assistant. Leave a message the first time that you call, explaining who you are and why they should cover your story. "Local resident makes good" is always a popular story in the press. Interesting angles relating to your work are also good.

Just because you get the voice mail is no reason to give up. Chances are that the reporters are too busy to return your phone calls. So try to call again, and again if necessary. Don't leave messages every time you call. That just annoys the recipient. If you do get the person on the phone, be sure to explain who you are, and give them the short two- to three-sentence spiel about your book. Explain that you have some local book signings and tell them about the book launch party as well. Your chances of getting an actual interview are much better if you speak to the person. If you present yourself as a well-spoken and professional author, then you've greatly enhanced the likelihood of getting on their show or having them write about you.

There are rules to follow for the different types of media events. Television is the most difficult to deal with. You have to both dress the part and sound like a professional. As we discussed in the chapter on press kits, make sure that the anchor has a copy of the questions for the author. This can be a big help. Presumably you've already done your homework and have witty, insightful answers to those questions. That takes care of the words. Try to dress well for the TV appearance. Watch the show if you can, and don't dress nicer than the anchors. You want to be on par with them, but you don't want to outshine them. This is their show, and you're the guest. So wear a white shirt, tie, and jacket if you're a man, or a muted dress if you're a woman. You don't want your clothes to be too loud or garish. Nor do you want to appear slovenly or too bohemian. Writers can get away with a certain level of eccentricity, but keep the quirks to a minimum. You want to intrigue the audience with your words and your books, not your appearance.

Since you're in a television studio, you don't have to worry about the routine concerns of home distracting you during the interview. You can focus on your television presence. Make eye contact with the camera often. Keeping your eyes focused elsewhere can make you look shifty or unsure of yourself. Make eye contact with the anchor as well. By appearing to chat with the anchorperson, you look more natural and relaxed —as if you've forgotten that thousands of people are looking at you.

Chances are that one of the staff, and not the anchors, vetted the book. So be sure to bring signed copies of the book for the anchor team, and then follow up with a thank you note to the programming director. You want to make sure to keep pleasant lines of communications open with these people, so be on your best behavior.

Radio interviews are slightly different than television interviews. In most cases, you'll be asked to do radio interviews live on the air with the hosts or taped beforehand. In either case, you'll most likely be conducting the interview over the telephone and not going to the studio. Most of the studios are cramped, crowded little places without a lot of room for guests.

Even though it's tempting to do the interview in your pajamas, treat the interview like any other business transaction. Dress the part, at least in nice pants and a decent shirt. While you might be tempted to be overly casual since you're at home, don't give in. Take the phone to a quiet room by yourself. Lock the door to keep out the interruptions and don't take anything to read or look at. Turn your complete focus on the radio hosts and what they are saying. Do not put the show on a radio in the room. It's distracting and the proximity of receiver and radio can cause feedback – the high-pitched squealing noise you remember from cheap microphones in high school. Even if you don't hear loud noises, you're likely to pick up the radio show as background noise while you're speaking. It's distracting to the listener, and you want the listener concentrating on you. As much as possible, keep your space free of any type of white noise so that your voice is the only thing heard.

Another suggestion you might want to consider is to stand during the interview. Not only does standing keep you more focused, being upright also helps with your breathing, since your diaphragm is unimpeded. This will give your voice a more natural and full sound than it sometimes has when you are cramped in a sitting position.

Radio interviews are normally fairly short, so make your points quickly. You're a local author, and you have a book out. It's available at such-and-such store, and you'll be signing there on this date. Those are the salient details to communicate in the interview. Beyond that, try to relax and sound comfortable. No one really likes the sound of his or her own voice, so try not to listen to the show as you are speaking.

Try to get on the station's morning show. The morning show is typically one of the highest-rated shows on any radio station, and will dramatically increase your audience. Most stations have a number of late night or early morning talk shows, but while you never want to turn down an interview, you won't bring in many listeners by appearing on off-hours shows. However, regardless of when or where or at what time you are interviewed, you enhance your chances of getting on the more popular shows by being a professional at any interview you do. In that manner, the producers can see that you show up on time, have something intelligent to say, and are articulate. All of these traits will add up to more interviews in the future.

Newspaper and magazine interviews are the easiest type to conduct, mainly because you're not committed to your words as soon as they come out of your mouth. You have the chance to edit yourself just as you edited your manuscript. This makes the interview easier for print. In some cases, the reporter will even ask you to answer some questions via e-mail. This is probably the least intrusive method of interviewing, and can give you added time to think up witty answers.

With magazines, ask to review the article before publication. Newspapers are on such a tight deadline that allowing you to read the piece would almost assuredly put them behind schedule. Most magazine journalists are not going to want you to review the article out of fear that you'll rewrite the piece in superlatives. Tell the reporter that you only want to verify the facts, not change any of the content. Some magazine writers will agree to this, giving you one last chance to check the veracity of the article.

For each type of interview, try to get someone to tape the television or radio spots or cut out the newspaper articles. Ask for complimentary copies of the magazine from the writer. Send copies of all your interviews to your editors. You want them to know that you're making a concerted effort to promote this book to the best of your ability. In some cases, when they see the level of commitment you have to publicity, they will start to consider helping with a media campaign. All of this will add up to more sales and make for a self-fulfilling prophecy: I work hard to promote my book; therefore my book sells more, which will convince my publisher to offer me more promotional assistance.

Another use for the interviews is to add them to your website. The majority of news media have an on-line presence that includes the news of the day and an archive of previous news stories. You'll want to wait at least 24 hours after the appearance of the broadcast or the printed interview to add the link. In some cases, the URL for a news item will change after it is rolled off of the current day's page and into the archives.

Many authors have a separate page on their websites that carries links to their news appearances. These links can refer people to print articles, radio broadcasts, and even TV news—most media is on-line these days via HTML or through different audio and video systems. Be sure to include links to reviews you've received from magazines and newspapers. Your readers, especially your biggest fans, will be interested in reading all your reviews. Adding links related to news appearances and reviews is another way to add new material and content in different media to your website. Plus there's very little time spent adding links to an existing website.

There's literally an entire world in which you can promote your book, but there are also many promotional opportunities that can happen in your own neighborhood. Building your reputation around the corner from your house can save you a lot of money in travel and expense. Besides, if you live in a city of one million people and just one percent of the population bought your book, you would sell 10,000 copies. That's a respectable number in almost any publisher's eye..

One particular promotional technique that works well when trying to build up local word-of-mouth about your book is to use flyers and posters. Also, be sure to leave promotional items in businesses in your neighborhood. People are more receptive to your book and your promotional efforts if you live just around the corner from them. I've gotten sales from people who stop by during a book signing to ask me if I'm local. If they can place where I'm from, it makes a difference.

For example, I put out bookmarks in the copy center where I printed and bound my ARCs. The promotion worked well. The staff at the store talked up the book to the other customers. They felt they had a more personal stake in the book, since the staff had helped in the production of the ARCs. When people came in to make copies, the customers saw bookmarks on the counter by the register. The staff explained that the early copies of the book were created right there in the store. Additionally, I put up a flyer in the window of the local pet store where I shopped. To place promotion materials in local stores, just ask for a manager, explain that you shop at the store, you are local, and you have a book out. Many of them will have never met an author, so be prepared for a barrage of questions. Once those are out of the way, in most cases, you'll be allowed to put the flyer on the premises.

Before I discuss what to put on your flyers or posters, here's a note about larger stores, particularly chain stores. Family-owned stores and small businesses are much more likely to help your promotional efforts than the national chain stores. Most chains have specific guidelines sent down from corporate headquarters on what can be displayed on the premises. So don't be surprised to hear the big names say no. However, the mom-and-pop shop doesn't usually have strict rules governing promotional materials, and since you've been a customer there you'll likely get the go-ahead to put up a flyer.

Like most of your other promotional material, the flyer should have a picture of the cover art, the title, author, ISBN, and the price. If you're well known in the neighborhood or have lived there for many years, you might want to consider putting a photo of yourself on the flyer as well. This makes the flyer more personal, and it will be more likely that people will pick up a copy of your book.

One final promotional technique that can be employed locally is the use of print advertising. Surveys have shown that print advertising is the most effective form of promotion for books. Most neighborhoods have a small press newspaper or magazine. So call some of your local publications and ask for their ad rates. In most cases, the cost for advertising in the weekly papers and local magazines are relatively inexpensive.

Additionally, while the sales staffs of small newspapers or magazines can't promise you a quid pro quo in which ad sales equates to editorial coverage of you and your book, they still might pass your name on to the editorial staff for a possible article. Since you are local and published, there's the tried and true article, "Local Resident Makes Good" story. Theoretically, the editorial staff has already been notified about your book via your press release, but this second, more personal way can often seal the deal. I've had a few instances where the mere suggestion of spending my ad dollars at a publication brought an article in the next issue. I'm not suggesting that you out and out lie to them, but in some cases, you will be advertising based on your promotions budget. The mere hint of purchasing an ad, whether you do it or not, can be enough sometimes to get an article published about your works.

Once you're satisfied that you've covered the local neighborhood, you're ready to go out there and start selling books.

Chapter 10
Authors on Parade

Authors continue to debate the efficacy of booksignings. Do they bring in people? Do they generate sales and new fans? What purpose do they serve? First, they do have one specific purpose. Each signing puts you in touch with the bookstores and the booksellers who will be representing you to the buying public. That's a point in favor of signings right there. Just by doing a signing, you've increased your book's sell-in (the rate of demand from wholesaler to bookstores) without signing a single copy.

Another point in favor of booksignings is that you get a chance to meet readers. This is an important task in selling books. Polls have shown that the majority of readers are influenced to buy books from word of mouth, and you can be the mouth that tells these people about your book. Most of the public doesn't read *Publishers Weekly* and doesn't watch BookTV (www.booktv.org). So they don't know what books are out on the market in any given month. Except for a few best-sellers, it's rare for people to hear when the next installment in a mystery series will be published. It's your job to inform them.

Setting up a booksigning isn't difficult. For the chain stores and the larger independents, you'll need to talk to the events coordinator. For smaller chain stores, it will be the store managers. For small independents, you'll talk to the owners. Just tell them that you're an author with a book just published and you'd like to come in to sign books. They will work with you to find a time to do it, and that's that. *call event's coordinator 3rd playback*

When you're setting up the signings, don't make any of them too close to the publication date. I know that you've been waiting for months for the day to arrive when your book is "officially" published, but in the publishing industry, the "pub date" is more of a suggestion than a firm date. You'll only add more stress to your life by worrying about whether or not the books will be available at the time of your signing. It's better, though maybe not easier, to wait two weeks to be sure that everything will be set.

You'll need to ensure that you have some media attention for the event. At the very least, you should put the signing on the events calendar for the local papers, both daily and weekly. Most papers have a section devoted to local arts events. You can submit your signing for their calendars. It's better to get more media attention if possible, but it's nearly impossible to do much in the way of media coverage for each event if you do more than one or two signings in your hometown.

If you do a series of signings in the local area, it's good to do some publicity with the people you know as well. When I'm doing five or more events in the local area, I'll print up some postcards and mail them out to my entire address book. If you've been following my advice, most of the people who you've met will be in a database by now. You can create mailing labels for the postcards and mail them out a few days in advance of the first signing for next to nothing.

Postcards for these events can be created from your word processing program and a box of pre-cut postcards. You don't have to be quite as fancy with these as you were with the cards announcing your book's publication. Leave the reverse side blank for the address label, and print up the cards with the schedule and clip art on the front side.

Another idea is to print up some flyers and hang them in shops close to the bookstores where you'll be signing. Keep the signs simple: along with the book cover, announce the date and time of the signing. Take the signs to stores in the area around your signing and ask the manager if you can hang up a poster announcing the event. Most stores have a place where you can post announcements, so you should have a pretty good acceptance rate.

Now's the point where I give all of you a peptalk about booksignings. I know authors who love them and others who despise them with a passion. There doesn't seem to be a lot of room for compromise when it comes to booksignings. Whether you like them or not, they tend to be a fact of life in publishing these days. While authors debate the worth of signings, most publishers expect their authors to do them. So chalk them up as part of the job.

At this point, I'm going to presume that you've called the store, talked to the events coordinator, and set up a date. Next, this might seem obvious, but arrive at the bookstore on time; in fact, you should arrive about 20 minutes early to the signing. That way, you can check out the lay of the land, and find the books and where you are located. In most cases, the store will have set up a small table, a few stacks of your book, and a chair for you. That's about all they'll do. It's up to you to decorate the table with things that will catch the eye of readers and to get noticed as people walk by. Sometimes, I won't use the table, but stand by it and talk to people as they come in. If you're tall (like I am), you'll attract more attention standing up than sitting. Plus you'll have the added bonus of a better chance at eye contact. People won't walk away as fast if you catch their eye.

Hopefully, you've been set up close to the door. Obviously, that's where the most traffic will be, and you are there to be seen. The extra time before the signing also gives you a chance to find the contact person and introduce yourself. You'll be taking some stress out of their life by showing up a few minutes early. Most coordinators put a great deal of effort into signings and want them to go well. They worry about selling books, and about making the author happy with the event.

If you're not by the door, check out the traffic patterns. At one signing, I was put in the salon area of the store. It was lovely, but no one came by. I moved to the front of the store and began selling copies immediately. Being put in a corner or off the beaten path is not going to help you sell many books. In fact, unless someone specifically comes looking for you, you aren't going to sell anything. That's not good. Chances are that most of the people in the store haven't heard of any of the publicity surrounding your event. The people are there to find something to read and you are one of the many options available. If you're in an out-of-the-way spot, talk to the events coordinator. Suggest a place by the front door or by the café. Some bookstore people are used to authors who don't want the spotlight. (We authors are known as a reclusive bunch.)

If you're next to an e-reader display at Barnes and Noble, suggest that they bring up your title as the demo book for the e-reader. It can help bring on sales to see your title on the Nook or other reader.

Just remember that you're in charge of your own destiny here. If you don't like where you're sitting, ask to move. You don't have to be rude or nasty, but just suggest pleasantly that you've found that you sell more books sitting by the front door. The bookstore wants to sell your books as well, so they normally will be more than willing to help you stand out.

Be polite and easy to get along with. Don't make any unreasonable requests of the store. You won't ask for a Waterford candy dish filled with only green M&Ms™. You won't ask for Evian water in stemware. You will not ask to be picked up for the signing in a limousine. This is not the time to exhibit prima donna behavior. Things you can expect to get from a store are something to drink (in the soft drink, water or coffee categories), a piece of chocolate or something to nibble on, and perhaps the store's courtesy discount on anything you want to buy in the store. Those are the reasonable requests.

I've never figured out how to determine how many people will show up at a booksigning. If there is a mathematical equation for determining how many people will show up to a bookstore on any given day, I have yet to find it. It seems to be some combination of other events in town, the weather, publicity, proximity to holidays, the weekend, the last lunar eclipse, and luck. The best you can do when holding a signing is to go in with a good attitude.

Of course, it helps to look the part of an author. While technically you can wear anything you want to a booksigning, I would suggest dressing slightly above average. I'm not advocating a tuxedo or formalwear. I believe that would make the customers uncomfortable by feeling underdressed for the occasion. You should wear nice slacks and a pressed shirt or blouse. Nothing denim, not cut-off, or too short. Shoes are negotiable since you'll be standing on your feet most of the time. You should wear comfortable shoes.

You should bring a pen, some of the postcards and bookmarks you had printed, and any other paraphernalia that you might think appropriate. One of the things you can do at a signing is make sure that people notice you. That's not to say that I'm suggesting that you throw yourself on the floor, kicking and screaming, though I've felt like it at a few signings. The idea is to draw some attention to the fact that there's an author in the store. The events coordinator should make announcements over the loudspeakers, and have a sign or two announcing your signing. The bookstore signs will typically not be as elaborate as the ones that you provide, but at a minimum should state the date and time of the signing along with your name and the title of your book. The same sorts of information that should be listed in their calendar of events.

Some authors have begun to bring a laptop and run their book trailers continuously on a loop. This saves wear and tear on the voice, because the book trailer will hopefully explain the novel and its concept. You won't have to go through the same patter for each potential buyer. However, beware. After 3 hours of listening to the same talk or music, you can go a little batty. Perhaps consider text for your video, and muting the sound on the computer.

You might consider bringing a few items with you to the booksigning to make sure things go a bit smoother. Bring a generic poster that announces the signing. A copy store can do this for you for less than $30. You can put your name, the title of your book, and the book cover on the poster for maximum effect. People are drawn to bright graphics. You can put this wherever you think it will draw some attention. Any small item that calls attention to you is good.

For the *Canine Crimes* anthology, I brought Beanie Babies™ to the signings. The little toys would bring the children running, and the parents would follow. It was a good way to start a conversation about the book. Plus I sold a few of the Beanies with my books as well -- a package deal. You can also bring postcards and bookmarks to put at the cash registers, so people will notice your books before they leave. You can bring a digital camera to take pictures with fans if they are so inclined. Also bring at least one pen that is comfortable to sign with, because you'll be using it a lot during the signing. The big grip pens or the pens with rubberized grips tend to be more comfortable than the standard stick pens. You can bring more if you'd like, but I've only run out of ink on one occasion, and then I borrowed a pen from the bookstore. I can usually pack all of this stuff into a backpack or a small duffel bag for portability.

You might want to consider bringing copies of your book with you to the signing as well. I know, you'd think that the store would have plenty of copies of your book, as that's the whole point of this event. Still, sometimes they don't. Or they bring in some books from your backlist and not the current book. Or the distributor sends the wrong title. All of these have happened to me, and these mistakes are not that uncommon. Putting a dozen or so copies of your book in the trunk will save you hassles and headaches. Most stores can arrange to pay you the standard price paid to the distributors (40 percent off the list price) or arrange to "swap" books where they order from the distributor and pay you back in copies.

Also, you should bring a blank guest book to the signing, like the ones at weddings. Leave it open on the table in front of you as you sign books, and encourage people to put their name address in the guest book as you sign their book. Of course as with everything else you do, you should add the names of the people who sign your guest book to your contact database. Since these people have already read one of your books, they are prime candidates for marketing your next book and every one thereafter. Marketers pay top dollar for lists of proven contacts; you're getting them for the cost of a simple guest book.

When you sign a book, you'll open the book to the full title page. That's the page that lists the title of the book, your name, and the publishing company. You can ask if the customer would like to have the book inscribed or just signed. If you do sign the book to someone, you should ask for the spelling of the name. You'd be surprised at the Tom, Dick and Harrys who spell their names Thom, Richard and Hary. A misspelling will mean that you have to put that book aside and sign another one. Then you should have some stock phrases to put with your signature. I tend to use platitudes like, "Best wishes," "Thanks for stopping by," "Hope you enjoy the book." Come up with a few that you can use. You'll need more than one because there will be cases when people buy multiple copies. You don't want to sign the same thing in all the copies going to a single person. Then sign the book. Some people say that you should strike through the printed copy of your name on the title page when you sign. I'm not sure of the reasons why some authors do this. I've heard this but again there seems to be two camps on this matter. Do what feels more natural to you.

Don't bring any other work to do during the signing. There will be times when you wish you had something to keep you occupied when you sit at the table by yourself. Don't bring a book to read. Don't bring another writing project to work on. Don't bring a crossword puzzle, or your knitting or your laundry to fold. For the next two hours, you will be the bookstore equivalent of the Wal-Mart greeter. Your goal should be to welcome everyone who enters the store. If they look at you and make eye contact, then ask if they like mysteries (or science fiction or romance or whatever genre the book falls in.) If they say yes, you have an opening to introduce your book to them in two to three sentences. If they don't respond to your greeting or don't like your genre, then wait for the next person and repeat the procedure. Some people will go out of their way to avoid you, but others will come over to see what the commotion is all about. And one gawker will bring more to your table.

I've found that inviting one friend to each signing is a good way to generate additional sales. For some reason, people are drawn to a signing if the author looks popular to begin with. When a friend stops by to say hello, you suddenly have one person standing at your table who is talking to the author. In almost all the signings I've done, that one person will draw others. I'm not sure I understand the sociological phenomenon behind that, but it works. When one or more people are standing there looking at your book, you become an author that might have a following (or maybe you just appear less intimidating to others.) I've joked about hiring a professional fan to follow me around to the signings and perform this function, but with a little planning, you can make sure to have one or two friends stop by during the course of a signing and bring on the crowds.

During the very slow times during a booksigning, the very worst thing you can do is expect that the world will beat a path to your door to buy your book. They won't. I can tell you that right now. You'll have to sell your book, just like any other product on the market. You don't have to behave like the shills who sell Ginzu knives or Ktel records, but you need to sell all the same. If you take a long, hard look around a bookstore, there are thousands of books competing for readers. You need to make people see why your book is special and worth the money they are going to spend. Except in the upper echelons of writing, people don't come hunting for your books very often. If someone makes a special trip just to see you, treat that person like gold.

Even in the worst of situations, you should try to keep a good outlook on the matter. You can't keep a running tally of sales as a way of measuring how well your book is doing. If you don't sell many or even any books on a given day, don't let it make you depressed. I've had days where I couldn't even get a person to look at my bookmarks, much less buy the book. It's easy to equate each booksigning with popularity and success, but you shouldn't. Every signing is a building block of your career. The forty people who walked by and read your sign, but didn't even slow down to say hello, are the same forty people who will remember having seen you the next time they see your book on the shelf. Some of them will mention your book to a family member who likes mysteries or history or whatever you write about.

And just like with building blocks, when you put down the first few, it's nearly impossible to see any kind of structure to them. You'll come home and wonder if you've made any impact at all with your signing. The answer is that you have. You just have to keep trying. After hundreds of signings, I can actually start to see some difference in the way that I'm treated when I go to a signing. But that's over ten years of doing the work of booksigning. I've paid a certain amount of dues, and still I get people who come up to tell me that they've never heard of my books or me.

Most of you will hear the dreaded mall signing stories of people who get asked where the latest Grisham or Harry Potter book is —or worse yet, customers will think you work at the bookstore and ask you where the bathrooms are. If you can, answer them politely, and then tell the person that you're really here selling your book. First, you'll change nothing by being rude to customers. Furthermore, you will make for some bad blood, because the store manager needs to sell books by all authors — not just you. So being rude about a mistaken identity will not endear you to the store. At one signing, a buyer was interested in legal thrillers. I introduced the man to Lisa Scottoline's books. He liked those books so much that he returned and bought one of mine because I had been so kind to help him. I've actually made sales to people who only wanted to ask me where the restrooms were!

While it's easy to want to be proud of what you've accomplished, there are many things that will knock you down to tell you that you still have a ways to go. At one convention, I sat next to Rita Mae Brown who writes a mystery series involving her pets. She has been writing for many years, and has produced wonderful novels in a number of genres, and has published several memoirs and books on writing. The signing line for Rita trailed out the door. I had two people in my line, but I stayed sitting at the table all the same. Why did I put myself through that torture? Because while those people stood in line waiting for Rita Mae, I talked to them. Some of them just noticed my name, but others took postcards and bookmarks. No one dared to get out of line for fear of going back to the end of the line, but they did notice me. So perhaps next year, they'll be standing in my line when I come back to the conference.

At the end of the signing, be sure to find the person who hosted you, and thank them for the signing. They had to go through a lot of work and expense for the event, even if no one bought your book. Even in the worst of situations, be sure to be gracious to the coordinator. It wasn't their fault. Most likely, they will feel embarrassed and be worried that you're angry about the lack of response. Reassure them that you had a good time, and talked to plenty of interested people who might come back to buy your book.

Then ask to sign some stock for the store. Most every store will say yes, because many people are intimidated by an author and come to the store later, hoping for a signed book. Even though I'm one of the least intimidating people on the planet, I still get people who are too shy to ask me to sign a book. You want the store to carry the book after you're gone. As long as it's in the store, it can be sold to another customer.

By signing stock, not only are you giving people who couldn't make the signing a chance to pick up a signed copy of the book, you're also giving yourself a free promotion. The books will be displayed with your name on them, and some sort of sticker or sign that you've autographed them. For local signings, see if you can get a few copies on the local books and author display shelf, which most bookstores, even the big chains, have somewhere in their store, but don't limit yourself to that category. The more places in the store where your book is displayed, the more likely it is to be discovered by readers.

Don't break down the display table before you leave. If you leave the table where it is, many stores will leave the display up for a few hours or days. Again this is just more publicity for your book, because the table will act as a presentation for your books. The prominent placement of your books is just another way to get recognition. Publishers pay good money for the endcaps (the exposed ends of bookshelves where books can be displayed) in a store for a reason

After the signing, you should send a thank-you note to the contact person at the store. A thank-you letter will help you reinforce your name, and remind the bookstore contact of how easy you are to get along with. Both of these are important to booksellers. You're in this for the long run, which means that you want to be invited back to future signings and events. If there's going to be a panel on writing in the future, the event coordinator will be more likely to include you in that discussion if you've been easy to work with in the past.

Another bookstore event that works well in conjunction with a signing is the reading group. Many of the larger stores have monthly groups that read and discuss books. The groups vary in size from five to fifty people. If you can have your book selected for a group's monthly reading selection, you can come in and talk to the group about the book and what was involved in writing it. Not only are you promoting yourself, you're practically guaranteeing that each person in the group will buy a copy of your book. These will be easy sales. Unless you're in New York or Los Angeles, most cities do not have very many resident authors; so having the author in to talk is something of a rarity.

As more bookstores close and other tighten their belts by reducing the number of signings they have, many authors have turned toward Book Blog Tours. As the name implies, the author travels from blog to blog, leaving a guest post on the blog. The posts can be daily weekly or however the author feels most comfortable.

The blog entries would ideally be about the author or the author's new book, so that the reader is well aware that the new title exists and is available for purchase. The author includes links to sales sites (preferably indie sites), the author's website, Facebook fan page, and twitter page as well. The reader can link in as much or as little as he/she would like.

You can give away books on the blog tour, where the nth comment or a random comment wins a copy of your title. It can be a way to drive more people to your blog entries.

There are many benefits to a blog book tour. For those who are shy or not people persons, this is a less extroverted way to promote your latest title. The interaction is limited to the computer, and perhaps comments on the blog. There's no face-to-face contact. Additionally, in this time of exorbitant gas prices, there's no cost of transportation. Blogs, like any prepared statement, can be edited, corrected and honed, so that the reader is only seeing the best of the author, not the uncensored, live version of the author. This leaves the reader with a better opinion in some cases.

JEFFREY MARKS

There are drawbacks to the Blog Book Tour though. It is just as time-consuming as the book tour. There are blogs to contact regarding whether or not they accept guest blogs and whether or not they would accept your guest blog. Try typing "blog" into Google, and see how many hits you come up with. It's daunting to try to find the best blogs for your story. MurderMustAdvertise has a list of blogs that accept guest blogs at its site. The excel spreadsheet is for members only, but for the reasonable cost to join (free), you can access the list of blogs willing to host.

Secondly, it involves a lot of writing. Granted, you are an author, but this is writing that takes away from your next book. Think of it this way, I've known authors who have written for 20-30 blogs and with each entry coming in between 600-800 words that can add up to a novella quickly. Add to the amount the fact that you have to keep each entry fresh and new. Nothing would be worse than posting the exact same entry 20 times. The reader would have no reason to follow you from blog to blog.

If you do decide on a Blog Book Tour, please follow the same types of etiquette that you would use for everyone else. Have your blog entries to the blog owner at least 5 days early. Don't wait until the day of the event or the night before to send them. If you've forgotten something, your entry will be late and the owner will be annoyed.

I've heard horror stories where authors sign up to blog on a particular day, do not provide the blog entry, and then do not respond to e-mails asking where the blog is. That type of behavior does not win you any friends. If you have overextended yourself or if something comes up, write to the blog owner. Be honest and explain the situation. There might be some annoyance at being left in the lurch, but it certainly beats the reputation of not responding to requests for explanations. Be sure to make sure that the date is correct. In these international times, 1/8/20xx, could be January 8th or August 1st, depending on the nationality of the person you're talking with. It makes a big difference in the due date of the blog.

The choice for a Book Blog Tour is yours. It is a way to reach readers and meet new readers without leaving home, but it can be time-consuming and organizationally challenging.

Chapter 11
Have Books, Will Travel

Bookstores are the most obvious, but not the only place, where you can go to sell books. Practically any store that sells merchandise or deals in books is a potential sales spot for your books. Library talks are a popular way to get new fans. Most librarians are big readers and enjoy having writers come in to discuss their books. Some authors turn up their noses at libraries because the books are borrowed and not purchased, thinking that there is no money to be made in the library system. That's a naïve approach to the American library system. Libraries are one of the biggest purchasers of hardback books. Tying into the librarians will help you to get into their system, and with any luck, get you into other library systems as well. Some libraries will buy multiple copies of your book for all the branches, or order multiple copies to replace the books that wear out. A typical hardback can only handle 50 checkouts before it needs to be replaced. While library patrons might not buy your book, the public library systems definitely are.

Library events don't have to be just about meeting librarians. You can also sell books directly to patrons at a library talk. In most cases, a "friends of the library" group will supply books for a signing after you give a talk. This is especially easy in cases where the library has a gift shop. Even if a library doesn't have a gift shop or a way to sell merchandise, most are more than willing to let you bring in copies of your book to sell.

So what does an author talk about when speaking to library groups? You can talk about writing or your genre or any other topic that the library thinks will lure in people. It has been my experience that more people will show up for a talk if the topic has something to do with the craft or business of writing. Fewer people want to listen to you expound on how you wrote your book, or the difficulties in researching a novel. I expect good crowds when I go out on the road for this book. People are interested in what it takes to be an author. If you choose to talk about writing, think in terms of what an audience would like to hear.

Some library groups will offer to pay you an honorarium if you speak. My general rule is to not accept a speaking fee from a library group if they are within two hours of home. I know that libraries are on a strict budget as a government agency. I generally would encounter no costs, except for a gallon or two of gas, in my work to them. If the library is more than two hours but less than four, I'll typically ask for travelling expenses, gas and a meal. If the library is more than four hours away, I'll ask for gas, meals, and the expenses required to stay overnight in the area. I don't plan on getting rich from my library friends, who have been big supporters of mine throughout my career.

Library association gatherings are a good way to break into the library market. As well as the annual American Library Association convention (www.ala.org/events) (which is the largest convention in the U.S. with over 25,000 attendees), each state and region has its own mini-convention. There is bound to be a gathering in your region, and you can attend for a small fee – or free if you can get someone to sponsor you. For most library conventions, be prepared to give away books. While this seems counter-intuitive, the harsh reality is that while most librarians love books, they are unable to afford many of them for themselves. So asking them to buy books (especially when they can check out books at the library without cost) is unreasonable. Additionally, conventions are notorious for giveaways and freebies. You won't get far by trying to sell your books in such an environment. By bringing a certain amount of giveaway books to a library convention, you'll be passing out books to librarians who will read them and then pass them on to be ordered by their library system. The easiest way to get library sales is through a review in the *Library Journal*, but attending the national ALA convention or one of the ALA regional conventions is certainly a wonderful way to get on the library's radar screen.

A local writing group is another organization that enjoys having writers come in to talk about craft. These are people who want to be in your shoes. You've made it, or so they think. You've written the book, found a publisher, and got on the shelves of the local bookstores. You have knowledge of the process that you can impart to them. For these groups, you should plan on talking to them about the publishing industry and any insights you might have gotten from the process. Since you're in the area, it is inspiring for these people to hear that someone just like them made it into print.

Thinking outside the box will help to get you into venues that you might not originally think of for booksignings. In many cases, you'll have to bring copies of your book to sell at these events, but you should already have some in the trunk of your car. Not only are you bringing copies, you'll be selling them as well. Unless you already have access to a credit card machine, I would not recommend taking credit cards. There are fees and expenses for accepting credit cards as well as a certain amount of hassle. For starters, you'd need access to electrical outlets and phone jacks to effectively take plastic. Cash and checks will do just fine. For most of these occasions, I round to the nearest dollar so that I'm not messing with change during the event. The worst thing you can do is to spend all your time fretting over the money, while you miss your big opportunity to make the sale. By rounding the retail price, you're focusing on paper money and avoiding any dealings with coins.

You'll be surprised at the number of places willing to have you come in to talk. I've done presentations at my nephews' elementary school on career day, talking about writing as a profession. I visited my old high school to talk to a creative writing class, and sold copies of my book there. I've sold books at county fairs, Civil War reenactors' events, and festivals celebrating Ulysses Grant. I've brought in reenactors in full Civil War regalia to perform skits as part of the booksigning event, as well. All of these are opportunities that can generate sales and new fans for you.

Stretch your imagination to consider that any retail establishment can sell books and hence can hold a signing for you. Try to find the obvious tie-ins with your subject and characters. Grocery stores have started to become a popular site for booksignings. Since the majority of book buyers are women and most grocery shoppers are women, there's a high traffic volume of likely buyers at the grocery. According to Bob Alexander, author of *Canis*, "you folks who aren't using supermarkets for signings are missing a sure bet. I sold a total of seven books at my first three bookstore signings, and had to donate three books as prizes. At supermarkets, so far three signings have amassed a total of 42 books sold. The traffic is much better than a bookstore."

Today most of the major chain grocery stores have a book section, so it's just a matter of talking to the wholesaler who handles the chain and then arranging the signing with the store manager. In most cases, the handling of the books in a grocery store is totally outsourced to a wholesaler, so you'll need to talk to the people who know the books. Stores only have to provide shelf space for the books.

Most managers are excited to have an author in the store, and you and your novel would be something of a novelty, since grocery stores tend to have very few in-house promotions. Drug stores are starting to fall into the same category as grocery stores when it comes to booksignings. Any pharmacy with a rack of books can be used as a backdrop for a booksigning.

The ubiquitous Wal-Mart stores are another place to sell your books. Most of the stores will ask you to supply your own books, and allow you to keep the profit. While this has good short-term value for you, it's better to work through the Wal-Mart distributor if possible. Although you won't make as much money up front from this arrangement, you'll have the benefit of being loaded into the Wal-Mart distribution computer application. With any luck, you can parlay that entry into their distribution system into being stocked in some of the Wal-Mart stores. This can be ideal, as the Wal-Mart approach is to go into smaller towns where the area is less likely to have its own bookstore. Hence, you've quickly added new markets to your distribution strategy. Of course, any of the other all-purpose discount stores can be used as well: Target, Meijer, CostCo or any local chain near you.

Be creative in your choice of venue. E. Lynn Harris went to black-owned beauty salons to sell his series of novels. Harris wrote of their world with the lives and loves of black women and a bi-sexual man. He knew where his audience was and took the books to them. Try to consider your audience. If you write food-related mysteries, think of doing a signing at a bakery or restaurant – perhaps a gourmet food store or a cookware store. All of these are possible sales avenues for your book. For other books, consider hardware stores, record and movie stores, theaters, pet stores, craft shops, decorators, hairstylists, gas stations, and computer vendors. If the books are related to a particular type of store, you've targeted your market and improved your chances for better sales.

This might sound oversimplified, but when it comes down to it, any store that has a cash register is fair game. Again, in some cases, you'll be asked to bring in copies of your book to sell, but with enough notice, you can get an appropriate number for the signing. Since the store will be ringing up sales, you will most likely need to bill the store for the books sold. If you don't have a suitable invoice form, you can pull a template from the Internet. Sites like Microsoft (www.microsoft.com) have business office downloads where you can find invoice templates. In most cases, you'll have to give the store the same 40 percent discount that bookstores receive when they order from a wholesaler. Even though many stores don't ask for an invoice, the typical accounting department expects paperwork from all its vendors. So if you know the exact number of copies to be provided, bring an invoice with you to the signing. If you're selling on consignment, make sure that you have the invoice out within five business days. You don't want the store to forget that you came in or, worse yet, think that because of the amount of time that has passed the invoice has already been paid.

For events where you need to supply your own books, it's best to buy them directly from your publisher. If you can, make sure that these books are counted towards your royalties. In essence, you are acting as a middleman, selling books to the general public. Some publishers don't want to count books that you purchase towards royalties, no matter if they are for your own purposes or for re-sale. You'll have to ask the bean counters if your efforts count towards the final numbers. The best time to address this issue is during the negotiation of the contract. Most of the major publishers still follow the old standard of not counting author sales as recorded sales available for royalties. I've found that more of the newer, smaller publishers are more likely to count any sales as a recorded sale. It's less of a hassle to have a single rule for sales, rather than making note of the source of the purchase.

Since you're acting as a middleman (similar to the wholesalers), your publisher should give you the same discount that they give the major wholesalers. Usually that is 55 percent. So not only will hosting signings in non-traditional venues get you more recognition from the general public, you'll be making a profit at the same time. Even if you give the stores their standard 40 percent discount, you'll be making 15 percent on each book sold. That can add up to good money when you're selling hardcovers.

If you're feeling generous with that additional cash, you can donate the 55 percent to charity by way of a fundraising event. You can provide books, and for each book purchased, you can put the money over invoice towards a worthy cause. You won't make any extra money on this type of sale. You will be selling books, however, and you'll receive royalties for the books sold. You'll need to work with a charity that you have historically been associated with or is associated with the themes of the book in some manner. The more tie-ins between you and the group, the better the chance for strong sales. As I've said, people like reading books that have a group resonance to them. Perhaps a friend or a person involved with the charity can hold the signing at their house, thereby cutting expenses for the event. You don't want to promote a charitable event, only to find that expenses have eaten away all the profits.

If you don't want to worry about the overhead for a charitable event, you can give the charity the books at cost, and allow them to sell the books as part of their marketing efforts. Girl Scout cookies are the most famous example of such charitable merchandising, but it happens all the time and in a variety of ways. School children sell candy and wrapping paper to friends and neighbors to raise money for their school. Why not your book? By just selling the books at cost, you'll get your royalties and be absolved of the chore of selling the novels around town. Plus you'll be building good will because you've involved yourself with a charity.

After a number of local events, you'll begin to feel as if you've mined your hometown for as much as it will yield. That means it's either time to go back to your desk to write another book or time to look at a more broad approach to selling your books. That usually calls for a national approach. Since you're on a budget, you'll need to make use of someone else's distribution channels. You'll need to find some organization that has the means to get the word out about your novel and to ship that book across the country.

If you look at the changing face of retail in America, you'll see that there has been a significant increase in the rise of catalog sales and at-home shopping cable stations. Both of these are perfect venues for selling books as well as cubic zirconia. When you look at your mailbox on the typical day, chances are that you'll find a number of slick catalogs waiting for you. One purchase from a catalog is likely to result in your name being sold to 20 other catalog mailing lists. You can bet if there's a special interest out there, someone has come up with a niche catalog to market to that group. All you have to do is find that catalog and pitch your book to the corporate buyer. Fairly simple once you find the appropriate catalogs. Of course, the Internet has made this process much simpler. There are a number of catalog aggregators listed in the Appendices of this book. Find a catalog that matches your area of interest and then pitch your book to the buyer using your media press kit and a copy of the book.

A similar process works for book clubs as well. Everyone is familiar with the Book of the Month Club, but have you heard of the Mystery

Guild or the History Book Club or Writer's Digest Book Club? All of these groups function in the same way as BOMC but have a narrower focus in what books they offer to members. These book clubs operate from a member list that will automatically receive a book every month unless the members send back a response card. If you can get your book listed in the catalog, you can be guaranteed hundreds of sales from this source. Obviously, it would be wonderful to be named as the featured selection of the month, but even being listed in the catalog can help your sales immensely. Some book clubs will want to reprint the books in their own cheaper format and binding. Others are happy to use copies of the book from a recognized wholesaler. There are literally hundreds of these clubs across America, and you can tap into them by researching clubs that might be related to your book. You can find a fairly full-listing on the Internet (or the library) via the Literary Marketplace (LMP, www.theliterarymarketplace.com) under book clubs.

Another venue that is becoming more popular is the at-home shopping networks on cable TV QVC, Home Shopping Network, and others sell merchandise on the air, allowing customers to call in with credit card information during a specified period of time to purchase a featured item. A number of authors have been featured on shopping network stations before, but be forewarned. This is not an easy market to break into and it requires a Professor Harold Hill-type personality to coax those people to part with their credit card numbers. Historically, bigger name authors and "star" books have been the best sellers on the stations, but there's certainly no reason for you to not try you hand at getting on one of these shows.

Of course, you can broaden your market by actually taking yourself on the road. So what happens when you decide to break out of your local area to tour bookstores outside your hometown? To start, you'll need to pick a location that you want to visit. If there's a particular theme in your book, you can visit an area that ties into that theme. I did a tour of the Southeast for *Magnolias and Mayhem,* which was a Southern-themed mystery short story anthology. Or perhaps you can tie the tour into an out-of-town convention or conference that you'll be attending. You should probably pick an area with a fair density of people. While the drive in Montana might be beautiful, you'd have to travel too far between each signing to make it worthwhile. If you have a book that pertains to farming or animal husbandry you might consider a rural book tour, but do so at your own risk. It can be difficult to find enough people to make the signing worthwhile.

After you select a place to go, you'll need to pick the timing of the tour. Pull out your calendar. Try to stay away from the Christmas season and major holidays in general. Many stores won't host authors at busy times of the year, for fear of clogging up already tight spaces. Give yourself enough time to visit a few cities, and slack time to drive from place to place. A tour will be taxing enough without feeling rushed.

Once you decide on a time and place, you'll need to determine what bookstores to visit on your tour. Just like you did for the local stores, research which stores host the most author signings and target those stores. You can look at the websites for the newspapers in the towns you'll be visiting to find literary events calendars. You can also ask for advice from people who live in the town. If you know authors in that area, you can contact them as well. Most authors are happy to help out and with sufficient notice, you can persuade some of them to come out to visit you at the stores. You might even be able to return the favor when they're out promoting their next book.

You're going to lose a certain amount of scheduling flexibility when you plan an out-of-state tour. You should draw up a tentative calendar for the tour, marking cities and dates for your planned stops. That will give you an idea of what dates to suggest to the store. If you're going to be in the city for more than a day, you have some leeway in the timing, but if you'll only be in town for one day, you're very limited in what times you can offer the store. Unless the store already has an event planned, most coordinators will be happy to work around your schedule in such circumstances.

You'll need to put more effort into promoting a non-local signing. The good will of your local signings will be lost because you won't be the local author made good. You'll just be another carpet-bagging bookseller passing through town. So you'll need to concentrate on notifying the media in each city. Call the television stations, send press kits to the local newspapers, and your tour schedule to the events calendars of both print and on-line papers. Your trusty postcards are a good way to get the word out to people you might know in towns you plan to visit, and don't forget to contact writers groups and mystery reading groups. . Finally, post the tour calendar on your website. You can create a Facebook event and invite local people to it. Do not invite everyone on your friends list. It's annoying to get 20 invites to stores that are hours away from your home. As I said, you'll need to do some extra work to make out-of-town booksignings successful because of the distance involved, but remember that you can make a success signing in any city you choose.

As I mentioned before, conventions and conferences are another place where you can sign books. The nice thing about these events is that they have a built-in audience, a fan base who has spent money to attend the conference. You're essentially doing an out-of-town booksigning, but you won't have to work the media quite as hard to bring in fans. They'll be coming to you. If you have time on the tour, visit a few bookstores in the convention area. You have a ready-made opportunity to stop by and sign a few books if they are in stock. If not, introduce yourself and your works. Try to get the buyer to order a few copies.

Before you spend the money to go to a convention, you should make sure that you are scheduled to speak on a panel or moderate a panel, and that you have a time scheduled for a signing. The panel lets people know more about you. As an author, you have a chance to talk about you and your work. Speaking on or moderating panels also allows for cross marketing by bringing in people who might have only come to listen to another author. In such situations, you have a chance to win converts.

Panels have their own etiquette as well. The trick is to be charming and gracious without dominating the panel. People will pick up on a microphone hog, and the sight will not make them want to rush out to buy your book. You should take turns and wait until other people are finished before talking. It's a lot like grade school. You should remember to bring a copy of your book to the panel to place in front of you during the discussion. You have a captive audience for 50 minutes. Make good use of it. They'll all be looking up to the front of the room where your book cover will be placed.

You should wear the same type of clothes to the convention that you wear to a booksigning. You'll find some authors who wear outrageous costumes or hats or theatrical capes. That may work for them, but in many cases, the author is better known for their drama than their fiction. Beyond the logistics of carrying this kind of costume to and from the conventions, you'll spend extra hours in preparation.

If you're participating on the panel, ask the moderator for a list of questions before the convention starts. Usually, you should be able to get them before you get to the conference. If you're the moderator, make sure to develop the questions and distribute them before the start of the conference. The panel assignments are made weeks in advance, and you should get a letter telling you who is on the panel and contact information for each of the panelists. This isn't *60 Minutes*. You don't need to be surprised by the questions —nor should you plan to spring surprise questions on panelists if you are the moderator. With a little preparation, you can talk about the topics knowledgeably. In my experience, you'll do better to talk about the subjects with some degree of accuracy rather than just pitch your books. If you're talking intelligently about a topic, you'll get more time to talk and people will be more interested in what you have to say than if you just repeat your ISBN to the crowd. I picked up one of Laura Lippman's books after she spoke eloquently about getting into the soul of a character on one panel. I wanted to see her book after hearing such depth in her discussion. I wasn't disappointed, and she didn't even have to specifically promote her titles to get me to buy one of her books.

The importance of booksignings at conventions almost goes without saying. You need a specified time listed in the program book, so fans can find you for an autograph. Usually signings are held just after a panel discussion, so fans have a bit of time to get copies of your book from the dealers' room and then come over to get an autograph. Even if you don't think that you'll have a single person in line for an autograph, go and sit in your assigned place. It's not because I want to see you suffer, but fans often come by with program books, magazines and other publications besides your book to sign. For years, I was asked to autograph a recipe that I included in a charity cookbook. You might not sign a lot of books —you might not sign any books —but you'll probably meet people who will buy your book after the convention just because they happened to meet you or heard you talk on a panel.

After the panel, be sure to walk around and talk to people that you don't know. You didn't come all the way to the convention to sit in your hotel room. Some authors don't spend any time at the convention, but all of the events at a convention give you opportunities to talk to people and possibly make new friends. As with panel discussions, you don't have to continually repeat your book title and ISBN, but just by the virtue of being you, some people will want to find out more about your novel.

Book fairs are another means of meeting fans. A book fair is a large number of booksellers and authors who come together to sign and sell books to a crowd of people. The events usually take place on a Saturday or over the course of an entire weekend. Usually admission is free or minimal, and customers can browse amongst the tables, looking at all the books. Book fairs are a great way to sell a number of books because all of the customers are there to buy books. As an author, you don't have to sell them on the idea of purchasing a book – they're at the fair specifically to buy books – you just have to convince them to buy *your* book. Since most of the people at book fairs come ready to buy, a good presentation means a lot to this crowd.

Each state or area usually has its own book fair. Look them up on the Internet and contact a few that are close to you. Some are in support of a literacy foundation or charity. Others raise money for a school or educational program. They are all run by volunteers, so be patient with them. They are readers, too, who want to make a difference. Most of them will accept you as a participant if you have had a book out in the past 12 months. Again if you can bring some items to your signing to draw attention to your booth, that's all the better. People will want to see what's so interesting and will stop by to check your books out at the same time.

As you can see from my suggestions, a number of venues exist to sell your books. All you need is the willpower to go out and make it happen. A few phone calls from now, you'll have a real book tour set up. Anything you set up in advance should be announced to the media via the press kit as part of your marketing strategy. Publicity tends to feed itself, and if people see that you're serious about promoting the book, they will make their own efforts to help out.

Make sure that any publicity events that you do set up are communicated to your publishing company. In many cases, the distributors will use your event information to make their stocking decisions. If you're doing 10 or more signings, you'll be more likely to get additional copies ordered into their warehouses.

Chapter 12
Onward and Upward

I wish I could tell you that it's all glory and fame once your first book tour is over. The normal amount of time that you should devote to booksignings is about three months per title. You don't want to wear yourself to a frazzle, and after that amount of time has passed, bookstores tend to look at your title as a book that's been out for a while. Even so, you'll never truly be done with promoting your own work as long as you can take a breath and write.

Usually within about a year of publication, the awards nominations will be announced for your genre. There's not a lot you can do to influence this process. You can ensure that your publisher (or you, if the publisher doesn't) submits the book for appropriate awards. I've got my fingers crossed that you'll be nominated. Fans of the genre vote on many of the awards, so if you've been doing your job properly and following the advice of this book, you have a good shot at least being nominated. Fans are more likely to recall a book whose author has contributed to other areas of the genre through personal appearances at conventions, articles in genre-specific publications, to name just two examples.

I've seen several cases lately where authors have tried to influence the nomination process through well-timed e-mails that reference their book and the nomination they are interested in. I would not suggest doing this for several reasons. First, this type of vote pushing is likely to anger the convention organizers. Remember these are the same people who will decide what panels you've participate on, whether it's with the bestselling author or the midnight signing in the broom closet. Also discussions with readers have shown that this process will turn off just as many people as it interests. That means that you're likely to lose a good number of possible votes. It's best to let the nomination process happen naturally and be grateful when your book is nominated.

If you are nominated, it's time for another press release. This release will be sent primarily to your local media, announcing that you've been nominated for your book in the best "whatever" category. Be sure to explain what the awards are, where the ceremony is being held and the date of the announcement. Someone who isn't familiar with the genre will need all of these details.

Of course, you'll be expected to attend the awards banquet. No matter how much it stresses you out or how much you'd prefer to hide out under your bed, you should plan on attending. If you want suggestions on how to behave at the banquet, just watch a few of the national awards shows, like the Oscars or the Emmys. The attendees smile, act like they are happy to be there, and spout lines such as, "It's an honor just to be nominated." You'll be saying and doing the same things. The last thing you want is to be perceived as is a arrogant winner or a sore loser. No matter how badly you want to win, no matter that your competitive nature has kicked into overdrive, don't show it. I've been nominated 12 times and won once. It never gets any easier.

If you win, keep your speech short, and to the point. Assume that by the time you receive your award, the banquet will be reaching for the three-hour mark, and people will be restless. I was at a banquet where people were so bored with the proceedings that they began to do the wave around their tables! Keep the picture of people hopping to their feet and waving their arms up and down in an endless circle fresh in your mind when you think of writing a speech that is longer than your novel. Thank the people who have helped you get to this point, and then be sure to mention the other nominees. No one remembers what you say if you keep it short. People will only remember your speech if you ramble forever – and you can be certain their memories won't be good ones.

Of course, if you do win, you'll send out a second press release, announcing that you've won. Savor the moment, and keep in mind that you'll probably manage to get some press out of the win. Media people are always interested in people who win awards. Next, take a deep breath, and allow yourself a few minutes of walking on air. You deserve it.

Of course, after you win you'll make sure that your award is prominently listed on all future dust jackets. "Agatha Award Winner", "Recipient of the Rockefeller Grant for Significant Writing", etc., should be displayed above your name on the cover. This is a good ploy for attracting readers. No longer is it just the author's friends who are saying that his book is worth reading. A group of judges have also given it the seal of approval. So this makes the book a safer bet for someone who has never heard of you.

You'll want to change your bio sheet and future references to the series, as well. Each future book in the series should have the line "Another installment in the award-winning Tom Jones mystery series" prominently displayed on the cover. Add a line to tell the reader that you've won awards for your work. If you're a mystery writer, give special heed to the Edgars, Agathas, Anthonies, and Macavities. If you're in science fiction, then it's the Hugo and the Nebula awards. It's nice to have won an award from your local writing group, but the more significant awards should be listed by name.

Once you've finished your tour and done the awards, you shouldn't rest on your laurels for too long. You'll need to start working on a new book. If you're in the mystery genre, you'll most likely be writing a series. People tend to invest in a character, and want to see what happens to him in future exploits. So you want to make the second book contain the same characters and some of the same themes.

Presumably your next book will find a proper home easily, and you'll be revving the motor on your publicity machine again. I wish that I could tell you that the process becomes increasingly easy as the number of books accumulates, but that's not necessarily the case.

With the booksellers you've established a working relationship with, you'll have an easier time setting up the next series of signings. You'll be able to get away with a phone call or fax to the events coordinator or manager. However, if you're going to visit new stores during an extended book tour or if you are planning signings at stores you've never visited, you'll have to go through the same steps that you did when you were starting from the ground floor with your first book.

I encourage you to spread your circle wider for each book you release. Do not abandon the stores that you've developed a good relationship with. You'll want to sign at their stores until you stop writing. However, with each new title, you should look for new stores and new venues to market your book. Don't get into the habit of visiting the same ten stores for each book. That's not the way to break out into a greater audience. You don't want to develop a relationship solely with one chain or one store, only to find it gone before the next book.

You can probably presume that the stores you signed with last time will carry your new title when it comes out. But the stores where you haven't signed might not have heard of you, and are not as likely to order your book. So go to the three stores that you've established a relationship with, and then look for seven new opportunities. Mix it up a little. Go to three superstores and maybe throw in a neighborhood bookstore for a change of pace. Not only are you combating the boredom that would set in from signing at the same 10 stores with every book, you're also building up a network of stores that will know you and buy your titles as they come out.

While you'll have to go through a number of the same steps with each book, you'll be starting from a higher place in your climb than you did with the first book. Some stores will recognize your name and call you about signings. Others will customers about your latest book if you've been into the store before.

In a similar manner, don't travel to the same places for your book tour that you did last year. Find another accumulation of bookstores that will have you and generate good sales – preferably in another part of the country. If you did the South one year, then do the Midwest the next. My first tour covered the Southeast. For my next book, I toured California, and next year I will be travelling through the Midwest. It's not just because I want a change of scenery. I want to attract the most readers that I can.

Before sending out the press kits for signings, you'll want to add one sheet of information to the press kit. That's a sheet listing your titles. The heading for the sheet can be something like "My titles" or "Titles for Jeffrey Marks" or "Works by F. Scott Fitzgerald." Then you should list the titles. The current title should be listed first and then the rest follow in descending chronological order. You'll want to put the title, ISBN, publisher, and price for each book on the page.

Why the emphasis on the previous titles? You're not done selling them by a long shot. You'll often hear an author's previous titles referred to as a backlist. These books actually start making money for you and the publisher. Ironically, if you go with a small publisher, many have made a concerted effort to keep backlists available and in stock. This can be a big help when stacked against some of the benefits of larger publishing houses.

I know from experience that your current title is the one that gets the most exposure and interest. There's a tendency for authors to take their older titles for granted, but don't neglect them. It's important to keep plugging your previous works as well as the most current book. First, you're increasing your chance to sell all your titles. Mystery readers are wild about series characters, so a continuing series means that any book could catch the book buyer's eye. And if a reader enjoys your current book, she might well decide to go back and buy the previous books in the series. So instead of a 1 in 500 shot on the shelves of the local bookstore, you're upping your chance to 2 in 500 or 3 in 500, depending on the number of books you produce. Each progressive title makes your odds that much better of a reader finding your books.

Not only can your current book help sell your earlier books, your earlier books can act as a hook for the current book. If a customer picks up your first book and likes it, then the chances improve that they'll come back to see if you have any more titles out. This can benefit you by encouraging the reader to purchase all of the books you have out, not just the current one. Of course, if you've been keeping track of your readers via cards, signings and other techniques, you'll have a database full of readers that you can contact about each additional title.

Many readers want to read a mystery series in order of publication as well. Many series are written in such a way that the most recent installment give away details of the earlier books in the series. While this is ultimately the author's choice, it can ruin some of the books in a series for readers. Imagine a book that you read where the love interest is the policeman. If you pick up an earlier book in the series and find the protagonist dating someone other than the policeman, you can pretty much determine that the other love interest is a victim or a killer in some book between here and there. While some readers are more than willing to handle this, of course, it gives away a certain portion of the story to the unawares. You want the reader to have good reason to enjoy all your books. This means that you'll have a built-in audience for your first book and subsequent titles.

All of these are good reasons why you should include a page in your press kit listing all your titles, and you should request that your backlist be ordered for your signings. Since most stores are interested in new books, if left to their own devices, they will just order the new book for your signing. That's the title most likely to sell in large quantities. I'm not saying that you should expect the bookstore to order cases of your old titles, but one or two copies can act as a catalyst. Many readers will treat you with a certain level of respect for having multiple titles out. A reader might think, "perhaps this is someone I should have heard of."

When books are still being sold at a relative steady pace, the publisher will most likely keep them in print. This is just another way of saying that the publisher will keep a minimal level of stock on hand and reprint the book as necessary when the current stock is sold out. Chances are that you won't make much money from your backlist, but I can guarantee you that you won't make a cent off a book that's out of print. This is yet another good reason to push for stores to order your backlist for your signings. Each booksigning should be used to maximize your sales and your career.

In typical publishing contracts, the rights to a book will revert to you after a certain period of time (typically two years) passes without significant sales, and without a reason to reprint. In this case, significant sales would probably be less than 20 copies in a six-month period. When a book is out of print, the distributor won't carry it and it will typically be marked as out-of-print. In years gone by this was the end of a book's life. Unless the author switched to a different publishing house and they opted to reprint your backlist, you might as well have buried the backlisted books.

Sometimes, a publisher will offer you a discounted price on the remaining copies of the book in their warehouse. Take them, by all means. The alternative is that the book will sell out in dribs and drabs over time. By taking the remaining copies, you can sell them at your signings and other events to promote your backlist as just discussed. The more books you get, the more you can sell at signings. Since you bought them at a discount and can sell them at list price, you'll be making a nice profit on the books.

Additionally, you'll want some copies to save for yourself and different events. I've heard stories from a number of people who didn't keep any copies of their book. Not only are they unable to enjoy their own successes, there are special events and circumstances that require a copy of your book, and you won't have one when you most need one. Additionally, you'll need to leave copies of your books for your literary estate. I've seen authors who have left a huge mess for their heirs. Books have gone out of print for the sole reason that the estate couldn't provide copies of the book to publishers. This is not the way to go down in posterity.

You should save at least one box of your title (about 30 copies) for special matters and for your own purposes. Don't sell these copies at your signings or give them away to readers. While it's not done quite so much anymore, some reprinting publishers want to see a copy of the book in order to set up the presses for the reprint.

While out-of-print used to be the kiss of death for books, it's not quite so anymore. In many cases, when the rights revert back to you, you have the option to sign up with an electronic book publisher or a Print-On-Demand publisher to keep your works alive. Currently there are a number of companies that will scan your existing titles and create a text document. This document needs to be edited carefully to ensure that any stray characters or unrecognizable characters have been corrected. Then the books can be uploaded to either Smashwords (www.smashwords.com) which covers most of the e-formats, including Kindle, or to Amazon (www.amazon.com) which solely produces books for the Kindle.

Please do not ask me to make predictions about which will be the reigning format next year or in five years. I point out that I was an early purchaser of a Sony Betamax, so I'm probably not the best person to talk to about formats. For the moment, I try to cover all the popular formats as to not lose sales.

There are also companies which provide page to e-book services for authors who are less technologically able. Kimberly Hitchens of Book-biz (www.bookbiz.net) provides full service and takes care of all the details involved in putting up your new e-books.

Some words of advice for putting up an e-book. You'll need to have a good cover for your book. Unless you have Photoshop or another commercial piece of software, it's probably best to leave this to the professionals. It's just as important if not more important than it is for print books.

You'll need copy, but if this is putting up an out of print title, then I would just suggest that you use the dust jacket copy of the original book. If this is a new title or if you feel that the copy is insufficient, then please spend as much time on this as you would a query letter to your first agent. It's the first impression that counts.

You'll also need reviews. Sometimes the on-line booksellers are savvy enough to tie the new format to the existing formats of the book, but in other cases, it appears to the casual eye to be a new title. In this case, you'll need to contact some on-line reviewers (see Appendix B) for reviews. These will help drive sales and announce the release of the e-book.

The on-line booksellers have mainly adopted the Facebook "like" option to announce your title on Facebook and other social media sites. By clicking on the button, it will post a link on your Facebook wall regarding the book. Getting friends to do the same will enhance your on-line profile and the number of people who might see the book.

Amazon also offers a Print-On-Demand service called CreateSpace (www.createspace.com). CreateSpace offers your out-of-print titles a second life in traditional print format. They offer a number of templates for you to use in creating the necessary files and a fairly helpful set of directions on the process involved.

While many traditional bookstores won't stock Print-On-Demand titles, Internet bookstores will offer the books on their websites, making it relatively easy to order them. One advantage of Print-On-Demand is that your titles are not out of stock when the print run ends. Since the books are printed on demand, you will theoretically never run out of stock. You can always request a few copies of the book to take to signings with you and you can also point booksellers to the e-publisher or P-O-D house to get more copies. As with the "in-print" books, bookstores are not likely to order many, but you'll improve your chances of having all the books of a series in print.

Chapter 13
Advanced Book Promotions Techniques

So far in this book we've covered the basic techniques for ensuring that your book gets a fair shake in the world. You've made the contacts, done the signings, and talked about your work on TV, radio and in the print media. Now we're going to look at some more sophisticated methods of getting your work before the public. In some cases, the techniques simply need more work or more thought before you move forward with them. In other cases, you'll need to use finesse in order to make the technique reap profits. And in still other cases, you might not want to use the methods, given your particular skills.

Many authors have started newsletters as a way of garnering attention to their work. In a world where some authors are putting out two or even three books in a single year, newsletters are a timely way to let your fans know what titles to expect from you next and when the books will be available. Your growing fan base can hear directly from you in a manner just as personal or impersonal as you care to make it. Some author newsletters read like the mimeographed pages stuffed into Christmas cards. Others are more like graduate school papers. My own newsletter, *Book Marks*, is published twice a year and has both scholarly pieces on US Grant, and fun pieces on what is happening with my life.

For most people, a standard four-page newsletter is sufficient to spread the word about their books. Four pages is an ideal size, because you can use a single sheet of 11"x17" paper folded in half. Four pages is sufficient space to give the readers enough information to find your books and enough news and other tidbits to get their attention, without writing a new novel on what you've been up to. You can find a number of templates out there for creating a custom newsletter in a variety of formats. Usually, the two-column format is the easiest to read and most familiar to your audience. Microsoft has a variety of formats that you can choose from on its website's download area.

So what do you include in your newsletter? First, you'll want a feature piece on your latest book, the one that is currently in print and you are promoting. This will appear on the front page of the newsletter, what would be the cover of the magazine, so to speak. If you're like me, you're always excited about your next book project, but on a practical level, you should be pushing the book that can make revenue for you now. That's your bread and butter. You'll want to jazz it up with perhaps a picture of you or a dust jacket of your latest book. You can also add some personal or family pictures if you want.

Beyond that, you should include a list of all your books in print. Again we're emphasizing the backlist of books you've published. Ideally, that will appear on one of the inside pages. Also on the inside, include one or two articles of a more personal nature. Include an article on a hobby or your pets. Show pictures of your pets. While this probably started as a tie-in to authors who wrote about pets, those pet photographs have become a staple of the industry. Include information on the inside pages that can't be found in your books: create a map of your fictional town; provide the reader with a family tree of a particularly complex genealogy. If your sleuth likes orchids or pottery or whiskey, provide the reader with some facts about his passion.

List any upcoming events on the inside pages of the newsletter. Being a good promoter, you should always have a list of at least a few signings and talks scheduled a few months in advance. This is a good opportunity to tell your fan base about where you'll be heading to promote your book.

The final page will be mostly blank, because most of the space will be used for the address. If done correctly, there's no reason to put the newsletter in an envelope. You can simply put the labels on the empty space created on the middle or bottom of the tri-fold. Print your return address on the back as well. That will save you the trouble of putting a label on each copy of the newsletter.

You can use the last page for finishing up any articles that ran over from the other pages. You can also use the last pages to list any upcoming titles you have. Provide some quotes, and reviews of the books as well as listing as much sales information (ISBN, price, publishers, and publication dates) as you can

If you have a decent word processing program and a good color printer, there's no reason that you can't create the newsletter on your own. The word processing file can create a camera-ready image that can be printed at home or by a commercial print shop. As we discussed, you can create a nice four-page newsletter from a single sheet of 11"x17" paper printed on both sides. Once the newsletters are printed, they can be folded, labeled and mailed.

While on the surface the newsletter project sounds relatively simple, there are several issues that need to be addressed – besides the newsletter. First is the cost. While you've done a good job of saving money to this point, the postage costs alone for this project can be prohibitive. If you consider this, realize that mailing just three copies of the newsletter will cost roughly a dollar. Multiply this by the hundreds of names that you've accumulated over the course of a few books, and you're looking at hundreds of dollars in postage alone for this project. You'll need to see if the cost is justified by the response to the newsletter.

According to Carole Nelson Douglas who writes both the Midnight Louie and the Irene Adler mystery suspense series, the newsletter is her most valuable promotions tool. "I've had the twice-a-year Midnight Louie newsletter since 1994. Newsletters are very expensive, but are the best way to build a mailing list of readers. *Midnight Louie's Scratching Post-Intelligencer* works because it isn't just about books, but about cats which is a way of tapping into a niche market. I've sold Midnight Louie T-shirts for some time. The modest amount of money this brings in helps underwrite the newsletter and builds community among readers."

You can ruthlessly pare down your list of addressees for a first pass at the mailing, but still it could end up being big money. You should leave the bookstores on the list, and all the fans that you've accumulated. You can remove the media people and others associated peripherally with writing, but the list will end up being longer than you expected.

Mail is going to be your best bet for a newsletter too. Although we discussed other, cheaper options for sending out a press release, those options are not as viable for sending out a four-page newsletter. First, you'll need to consider those graphics. While they might look good on your computer screen, they will only reproduce as well as the fax machine on the other end of the line. That means that you can end up sending huge files that take ages to transmit, only for your readers to find a black square where your wonderful graphic used to be. So consider a pared down newsletter if most of them will be going out via fax.

You also have to be careful with e-mail newsletters as well. A four-page document attachment with graphics can run into several megabytes of data. This could be more than some servers can handle and in other cases, it might fill up a reader's mailbox, so that they can't receive any other mail. You don't want to be responsible for taking down someone's mail service with your newsletter. You'll want to keep your graphics to a minimum when you're sending the e-mail newsletters. While it might look better with that high-resolution photo of your dog, and your new book jacket, you'll be dramatically increasing the size of the file you transmit. A better bet is Adobe PDF, which creates a read-only file that typically is only a fraction of the size of the word processing document.

In some cases, e-mailing a newsletter to your mailing list is considered "spam," unwanted e-mail from a commercial source. You'll need to make sure that your Internet service provider allows large amounts of e-mail to be generated from your account. AOL is one provider that does not. If your service provider does not allow mass e-mailings and they catch you, you could be contacted by the provider for an explanation and, in some cases, even booted off the service. You can avoid this potential conflict by only sending e-mails to the people who are on your mailing list and have signed up to receive your newsletter. There are commercial services that allow for e-mails to a mailing list and take care of managing your mailing list for you, which can allow readers to opt out of receiving more e-mails.

Some authors have gone to text-only e-mail messages. There are no graphics, but sometimes there are links to other pages for graphics, additional info, and even on-line booksellers. Everything is in text, within the body of the newsletter, but set off by simple ASCII characters. Zero attachments, in other words. In an age where every attachment can be a virus or worm, this approach offers a way around that. Another plus is that text files are relatively small and can be sent faster.

If you are sending e-mails yourself, as a courtesy for your readers, you'll want to make sure that you list all your e-mail recipients on blind copy. This means that the person opening the e-mail will see your name as the sender, and their name as the receiver. No other names will be seen, no matter how many copies you send out. This prevents any other person on the mailing list from responding to everyone on the list, and creating an e-mail nightmare. It also acts as a privacy protection, though you'd hope that no one actively denies reading your books in public.

One thing to remember with bulk e-mail is that the market is becoming heavily regulated. That means you'll have to comply with a host of government regulations in doing this. You'll have to provide some sort of opt-out process. That means you have to have some way of letting the users out of receiving future copies of your newsletter. Not only is this common courtesy, this is also mandatory at this juncture. Of course, many bulksters get away with this by slightly changing the sender's e-mail for each mailing. So there are ways around the regulations. Also you'll need some mechanism to show that you didn't do send this e-mail randomly. If you save your contacts list, you'll be fine on this count. You don't want your newsletter or announcement to be presumed to be "spam". You want it to be read and enjoyed by the people who you have dealt with in the past.

There are programs and mechanisms to help you write an on-line newsletter. One of the best tools I've found is located at www.authorsden.com. The site is specifically geared towards writers and readers. The site continues to add new features, but one of the nicest options is their newsletter administrator. The site has a place for readers to sign up for your newsletter, and also provides HTML code so that you can add readers from your website. You can then go directly to the Authorsden site and send out a newsletter. The program to do that is fairly simplistic. There's no special fonts or types, but you can add links to your site or to places on-line to buy your book.

Vertical Response (www.verticalresponse.com) is another site that you can use to send newsletters and reminders. Several major authors, including Lawrence Block, use it as does the Mystery Writers of America. It has the same features as Authorsden, but has HTML code available for double-opt in on signing up for newsletters. Vertical Response also allows users to opt out in the e-mail, which is a must for your newsletter not to be considered spam.

There are other similar sites that provide this function. You should probably try to stick with one of them, rather than opting to go it alone. That can be time-consuming and frustrating. With new regulations expected in the area of bulk e-mail, this would tend to be the best option as e-mail utilities will be updated by the websites, allowing you to do what you do best, and not code HTML.

There are currently services that offer to send out ads and information about your book to thousands of readers. The ads appear in on-line newsletters and link to your website. I would not suggest using their services. They typically charge close to $1000 for the service, which is extreme, considering that we've been doing most of our communication for a few dollars. I never advocate any service that charges more than $100 for communications or clicks. Most people that I've spoken with have not converted those clicks into significant sales. If your publisher wants to purchase the service, great, but I would avoid using your promotional budget to do so.

I also include a link to my newsletters from my website. On the "news" page of my website, all the past issues of my newsletter are available for anyone to read. This is a convenient way for anyone who does not wish to receive e-mail, but wants to keep up with the newsletter, to do so. You can create a "Note" on Facebook as well and put a text copy of the newsletter there as well.

One way that you can increase the number of e-mail addresses you possess is through the effective use of giveaways. So many people think that free books grow on trees or that publishers supply their authors with unlimited supplies of free books so that they can sprinkle them across the country like a literary Johnny Appleseed. You'll be surprised at the number of people who will ask for one. The only time that you should really give away books is when you get something in return. Whether that is publicity or contacts or other consideration, you shouldn't feel obligated to pass out freebies unless you're getting something in return. Every book that is given away is one less sale for you. You should keep that in mind. Even so, most publicity budgets will show that the cost of promotional books is the biggest expense you'll incur. Even at a 55 percent discount, you'll still be charged about 10 dollars per hardcover. That will add up quickly.

So how do you make sure that your books are going to good use? Obviously, the free books sent to bookstores to show them your book prior to setting up a signing are good. Still, there are other opportunities to get something for copies of your book. One of the most common approaches is to run a contest or drawing for free books. The idea being that in order to contact the winner, you'll need to have contact information about the people entering the contest.

Of course, you'll retain all the contact information that you receive from the people who enter the contest and input them into your fan contact database. This is a good way to get a number of additional fans for your promotions. Everyone wants something for nothing and all the Internet sites asking for contact information have desensitized most people to giving out personal information to strangers

Recently I held a promotion for a book giveaway. I promised a free copy of my biography of Craig Rice, and a Craig Rice novel to someone who signed up for my contest. All the entrants had to do was go to my website and sign up for my free newsletter. The contest served a double purpose. First, it rapidly increased the traffic to my website. Even though the sign-up for the newsletter was on the home page of my site, I found that traffic to *all* pages went up dramatically. Once you get people out of their inertia, they tend to look around at your website. The second purpose was more obvious. I got a list of people to add to my newsletter mailing list. Contests help authors increase their name recognition, which can be reinforced through newsletters and mailings. While every person on your list might not like your books, certainly they have friends and family who might be interested in your book.

Name recognition is another reason why you can give away books and still come out ahead. After all, there are many potential arenas for giveaways, which allow an author to reach a large number of potential readers. Think of donating books to a charity auction. Our local PBS television station has an annual auction to raise money for their operating expenses. It's also one of their biggest ratings draws. Think of donating autographed copies of your books to such an event. You'll get plenty of free publicity as the announcers talk about your books and start the bidding. And don't forget to take the expense off of your taxes under charitable contributions.

Knowing how much appearances count in the world of marketing, don't just fork over two or three copies of your books. Make an event out of the books. I usually put the books in a small basket for display purposes. I'll throw in some postcards, bookmarks, and whatever other promotional items I might have around. If the book has a distinct theme, you can add a small item to give it some flair. For promoting my Grant book, I've included Confederate money, Civil War non-fiction books, and airline -sized bottles of whiskey. All of these things make the buyer stop and take a long look at what all is included in the auction. The more the package is studied, the more likely it is that the bidders will remember your title. As you prepare the basket for delivery, you should consider shrink-wrapping it. It's an easy process. Wrap the basket with the clear plastic wrap and add heat, usually through a hairdryer. This will help you in getting the package ready to ship and to keep curious fingers out of the goodies.

Beyond asking for free books for themselves, you'll find that many people want to ask for books for their favorite charity as well. In the most likely scenario, you'll be asked to give signed books to a worthy cause. Take a good look at the cause, and how it can help you. Just like you don't give money to everyone who asks for it, you can't afford to give copies of your book to everyone who asks. You should look at the circumstances and the potential for cross marketing. If the cause is near and dear to your heart, by all means donate. If not, then see if there's an angle that can be played. If you're not familiar with the cause or are ambivalent about it, then you can find out how the books will be sold. Is there an auction list with advertising? Maybe you can get a free ad for donating your book. For the canine anthologies I edited, I gave some signed copies to the SPCA for their annual auction. A nice tie-in since I assumed everyone would love dogs and want to read about them.

For these events, you don't have to go all out. Just a signed copy of the book and a bookmark should suffice. While it's easy to get carried away with creating a basket for giveaways and auction, you should save the fancier baskets for when the audience is likely to examine the baskets carefully before the event. Remember to get a receipt for the each of the auctions, so you can declare these on your taxes. Additionally, see if you can get the contact information for the winner of the auction item, so you can add them to your list of fan contacts for later events and drawings.

Once your website is operational, one of the ways to generate more buzz about your Internet presence is to add what is called interactivity. That's the concept that a web surfer is more likely to come back to a site repeatedly if there are activities that require his input into a situation. Those little polls on all the major search engines are not the mere whimsy of a HTML coder. The idea behind polls on websites is to give the web surfer an idea of the major issues of the day and to let him vote on them. The same with puzzles and contests. All of these require the user to do more than just read text they become active participants in the site.

So how can you get your site to be interactive? First, realize that it's going to take a certain amount of time from you or a friend who maintains the site. It is very expensive to hire a person to maintain a site on a daily or weekly basis, and you'll need to devote at least a few hours a week to this endeavor. Nothing looks worse than having the same poll out there for eight months. Things have to appear fresh and current.

One of the cheapest and easiest ways to make a website more interactive is through the use of message boards and on-line chats. Message boards, like bulletin boards before them, are merely a place where people can write or "post" messages on your website. In this situation, if the readers are asking questions of you, you have the ability to post an answer to the question for readers to see. This can take the place of Frequently Asked Questions (FAQs) pages that are normally included with a site. Alternatively, you can chat with your readers on-line, in a manner similar to that of the chat rooms. All you'll need is some software that can be downloaded from a number of on-line sites. After that, it's just a matter of posting a time to get together to "talk" (or more to the point, type) with your readers. Be sure to take time zones into account and post all chat times with the appropriate time zone, as well.

Push technology is a new means of getting visitors back to your website. The information on your site is "pushed" to the user via an e-mail informing them of updates to your website. Several services, including RSS and Digg It, allow people to subscribe to updates to your site. RSS stands for really simple syndication or rich site summary. Syndicating is legally publishing an article from your site elsewhere on the web.

There are benefits to using RSS. It allows users to get the latest updates without surfing the Internet. It gives the power to the reader. It lessens inbox clutter, and it is spam free. Unsubscribing, a major legal requirement these days, is easy to do.

Of course, it can be used as a marketing tool, which is why we're talking about it here. It targets your marketing to readers who are interested in your book by sending the latest news on products and services.

As Beth Tindall of Cincinnati Media explains, "Let interested individuals tell you they're interested in getting your newsletter or an alert when your website has been updated, or get first crack at a contest, whatever it might be…let ConstantContact or YourMailingListProvider or Vertical Response manage your mailing list —individuals subscribe/ unsubscribe and you don't have to constantly add/change your address book or groups to mail to. Let technology do the work for you — it does it better when you manage it right."

The term podcast comes from the iPod, a listening device that allows billions of bytes of sound to be stored on a tiny device. Podcasts are downloadable broadcasts that can be heard on most MP3 players and iPods. Authors can use podcasting to create content that readers can download and listen to at their leisure.

Historically, most podcasts were radio feeds and interviews, but new technology makes it easy to create your own podcasts. The first thing you'll need is a microphone. I'd suggest using a USB mike, which can be purchased for as little as $50. They plug right into the computer and can be used to make your podcasts.

You'll need software to record and create podcasts. Audacity has free software to record podcasts, but of course, free means not professional quality. Goldwave Digital Audio Editor can be purchased for $50 on-line, and is an improvement over Audacity. Cubase LE is a better package and is included with many recording interfaces for computers.

Once you've created your podcasts, you'll need to include a link to it on your website for people to find. You can also list the podcasts with podcast directories like podcast.net, ipodder.org, and podcastalley.com.

You can also add podcasts of interviews you've done. Sites like Gelati's Scoop and Suspense Radio have large followings and can help to increase sales.

In addition to promotions for the ears, we now have promotions for the eyes as well. Video book trailers have become all the rage. These are promotion tools that can be used to promote your book on some of the many video sites that have popped up on the web, like YouTube. In the same way that trailers promote a new movie, book trailers promote the release of a new book by sounds and pictures.

Like many things in life, there are two options in creating a book trailer. You can create your own or have it professionally done. If you choose to do your own, software like VideoSpin or Windows Movie Maker exists which can help out. You'll need to decide on the graphics to be used, the captions for the photos, and the timing of each slide. Many homegrown videos will try to run the captions so fast that Evelyn Woods could not read them or time each slide for the same amount of time, creating a monotonous timing. Play with the timing (which should be under 2 minutes to keep the attention of the viewer) and length of each slide. Ensure that there are transitions between slides and ideas. Use a photo of you, the book you're promoting and any other public domain images that help promote your book. For my US Grant series, I've used photos of Grant and Civil War battle scenes. These go well with the text that I have included to help explain the book.

Public domain music can be used in the background, but don't make it so loud that it rattles the keyboard. The music should be in synch with the images. For the video of my Craig Rice biography (http://www.youtube.com/watch?v=t_yGBPFDg18), the music is an upbeat ragtime piece, which stops suddenly when the slide appears telling about Rice's descent into alcoholism. The change is ear-catching as well as eye-catching. If you have a friend who writes or plays you might decide to choose a song by him to use as background and then cross-promote between the two arts.

You can use voice over in your trailer as well. You'll need a good microphone and recording software. I strongly recommend doing this as the very last step of the process if you do. You'll want the timing of the images to be precise before you start recording as you want your voice to match the photos in the video. It looks terrible to talk about the cover 20 seconds after the cover has transitioned into another image.

However, the homegrown versions are typically to the point, about the book, and easy on the pocketbook. You can produce a nice trailer for less than $100 including software in most cases. Windows Movie Maker is now free on most newer computers, so the cost is negligible and may be limited to any non-public domain images or music licensing.

Professionally done trailers are more stylish and polished. They typically use specially made videos that interview the author and can use a variety of images outside the scope of what an author could do alone. However, as with website flash intros, they can be slow in loading, and with videos, this leads to long pauses while buffering takes place.

While most trailers are seen on-line, some authors have said that they now show their videos at book signings. One of those personal DVD players can be used to show the video in an endless loop, which can be of interest to readers passing by as well as saving the author's voice.

Most video trailers are posted to YouTube. YouTube has HTML code that can be used to link to it from any website. So you can then use the link to connect the video to your website, your profile on the social networking sites, your blog and other on-line venues.

There are other ways to get more return visitors to your site. As mentioned before, polls are one way to do this. You can poll readers on the title of your next book, or where they would like to see a series go, or any character that should be given a larger role in an upcoming novel. You can also have contests on the site. You can get fancy and have on-line quizzes that will submit the names of the contestants for a giveaway if they answer a certain number of questions correctly. Be sure to collect all the pertinent data from the contestants so they can be added to your contact database. Polls and quizzes are timely matters, and you'll have to make sure that they aren't open too long or readers will start to get the idea that the site has been abandoned. I ran a contest, a book giveaway. The contest was much easier than some competitions. All it did was require the players to sign-up for the newsletter on my site. From that list of people, I gave away copies of the book. It was that simple, and I got a list of names that can be used to promote my books via a newsletter. You can also encourage readers to join Internet communities from your site, and pledge money to special causes. There are a number of ways to get people to come back to your site, but your site must always be updated on a regular basis.

One technique for giveaways that I've used with great success is to auction off the name of a character in a book. This freebie will cost you nothing and has the potential to raise a great deal of money for charity. You'll always have a few minor characters that can be named anything you choose. Take one of them and name them after the winner of the contest. Not only will the winner be likely to buy several more copies of the book, you can create another press release announcing this promotion and its contribution to charity. You can get a lot of mileage out of this technique.

I've also created baskets of books for other auctions. Most of the major conferences have auctions that support local charities or help keep the conference afloat. I create a basket of goodies that help a good cause and get my name out there. I typically do a themed basket of books around a particular author whom I've profiled or perhaps my own novels with some hard tack or perhaps a biography of US Grant. My local PBS station has a yearly auction to help support its work financially, and if you donate more than $150 (the cost of a few hardbacks these days), you have your basket and your name mentioned during their advertisements for the auction, creating even more publicity. For sheer size and contents though, I must say that the romance conferences put the other genres to shame. If you're going to a romance conference, the basket needs to have bows, shrink-wrapped cellophane, comfort items like scents, soaps and body powder or chocolates, teas and other nibbly items.

Another practice that is becoming much more common is the group signing or the group tour. There are a number of reasons to sign as a group. First, you're more likely to bring in more people as part of a group. You can sell copies of your work to other readers who have come in to see the other authors, similar to the idea behind panel discussions at a convention. The additional people are a plus, and additions are always welcome to any signing.

An additional benefit to group signings is that you're suddenly part of a local signing group in multiple locales. Each of the other authors has a local signing base, a number of fans, and a list of contacts that you can use to get your books stocked in other stores. The other authors should be willing to pitch your books as well as their own. A signing group is not a competition, and the book-reading public should not be looked at as a pie, in which there are only a few pieces to go around. There's more than enough "pie" for all of us. If you remember that maxim, you should have no trouble getting along in a group-signing situation.

Besides bringing other people to the signing to keep you busy, it's nice to have other authors around to talk to when the signing is slow. They can keep the boredom away while you sit there praying for someone to walk through the door of the store. Misery loves company, and it's nice to have another person there to share the misery "pie" with. If you're touring in another part of the country, you'll have someone to eat meals with and someone to travel with. It's a nice feeling to know that you have a support system right down the hall from you should anything go wrong.

The group signing or tour method can also save you money. If you're traveling together, you can share expenses on rental cars, hotels, and food. You can pool money for advertising and press kits. You won't be shouldering the entire burden by yourself.

You will need to be careful though. You want to find people to travel with who you're compatible with, professionally and personally. You want to be part of a group that has somewhat similar characteristics in their fiction. If you write humorous soft-boiled mysteries, you'll want other funny authors. If you write serious historical mysteries, you'll want to find other writers from different eras. Try to imagine Agatha Christie and Patricia Cornwell traveling together on tour. Despite the obvious draw in pure sales figures, they are not well suited. It's highly unlikely that a Christie reader is going to like Cornwell and vice versa. Their works are too dissimilar and no synergy is to be gained by traveling as a pair.

Once you find authors who match your style and personality, you'll need to come up with a catchy title for the group. As authors, you're always expected to be clever and witty. This will be no exception. You should find a name that you can live with for a while, since you're likely to be doing this for quite some time.

You'll also want to make sure that you're compatible on a personal level. Touring together is like marrying into someone's family. All of a sudden you have these people that you're stuck with for weeks of travel time. Be sure to choose them wisely. Besides the proximity in touring, you'll also be sharing resources. You'll want to make sure that it's a good working relationship, because essentially you trust them with your money and your career. You might want to take a trial signing or two on, just to make sure that you'll be good working together.

I've been fortunate to travel with Kris Neri and Julie Wray Herman. Julie and I traveled together one year and Kris joined us the next. All of us write humorous, cozy mysteries. While none of us write close to the same vein of books, we certainly could all be put in the same subgenre. As a result, we decided to tour together. All of us have a reddish tint to our hair, so we quickly became the Red Headed League. We've had a lot of fun with the concept. We've listed "Miss Clairol" on our signing tour brochures, and we've thrown in bottles of hair color into some of our giveaway baskets for a dash of humor. It lets the reader know that we're fun, and they should expect the same from our books.

Even though I'm the one writing the book on promotions, I have to admit that I've learned a lot from Julie and Kris. They have shown me a number of techniques and ideas that I hadn't thought of on my own. Julie has had some ideas listed in this book. Kris teaches a class on how to write mystery fiction, and is a wealth of knowledge on the genre. Kris has the added insight of owning a bookstore in Sedona, Arizona. I've been able to incorporate the ideas into my solo signings in order to sell more books.

Additionally, we've been able to do a lot more print advertising than I would have been capable of doing myself. Last year, we chipped in for the back page of the Malice Domestic program book. It would have been a significant investment for one of us, but with all of us throwing money into the pot, my portion was only about $125. That's certainly within my promotional budget.

We've also tried some new techniques with us as well. By doing our own individual signings, we're making sure that the stores carry each other's books and we put out promotional materials for the others as well. So now if I'm on a deadline and can't make a conference, I can count on Julie or Kris (if they are attending) to put some collateral out for me. Suddenly, I'm getting three times the publicity I was, even when I'm staying home.

Another promotion technique for authors who are not feint of heart is print advertising. Of all the advertising venues open to authors, print is the most effective media for getting results. The number of options for print advertising is mind-boggling, though. Think of the number of newspapers, magazines, and publications – all striving to get your money. You'll need to do significant amounts of research to make sure that the money is well spent.

There are a few rules of thumb. First, don't spend huge sums of money on advertising. It can help promote your book, but by itself, it won't sell books. You don't want to skew your budget to print advertising to such a degree that you don't have money for tours or postcards. As a general rule, I try not to spend more than $500 on any one ad or promotional opportunity. That keeps me in line with spending on the other areas of promotion.

And always remember this: don't accept the ad rate guidelines as written in stone. Just because it's on paper doesn't make it real. Ad men want to sell ads and want to sell as many as they can. Often that can only happen when they shave a few dollars off the price, so feel free to bargain with them. Maybe you can get some special placement or promotion with the magazine to make the deal sweeter.

Generally, the more specific the publication, the better your chances of making the advertising money work for you. A general magazine, like *Time* or *Newsweek*, may be great for reaching a large number of readers, but unless they are interested in your book, it's not money well spent. You'd be better off in printing an ad in a smaller publication with a much more focused audience that would be interested in your writing.

You don't want to print an ad in a sewing magazine unless your book has something to do with sewing or unless you're rather well known in sewing circles.

There are a few places where an ad can do something for your sales. The first is any publication that is associated with your genre of choice. For the mystery world, that includes magazines like *Deadly Pleasures*, *Mystery Scene*, and others. For romance, it's *Romantic Times*. Go after magazines read by people who love your genre. This way, you know your audience from the start. You know they like the type of book you're selling if they are reading these magazines.

The next place where you should consider advertising is any trade magazine related to the topics in the book. If your hero is a military veteran, consider advertising in a military magazine with an ad slanted towards that aspect. In *The Ambush of My Name*, the protagonist is Ulysses Grant. Any of the magazines dedicated to the study of the Civil War are fair game for my print ads. I know that people are interested in Grant from a historical military standpoint. Therefore, they are a good target audience for my book. If your protagonist is physically challenged or has an interest in a specific topic, you can use that to advertise in the trade magazines for that industry. Everyone likes to see his or her areas of interest covered well in fiction.

Another place where advertising might do some good is in the program books at the major conventions. The ad space at the conventions is reasonably priced and, again, it's an audience that is interested in books in your genre. These people have actually paid to come see their favorite authors, so not only do you have a captive audience, but one that is ready to buy.

Be sure to count in all the costs for printing an ad. You'll be quoted a price on the ad space, but don't forget to add in costs for color, cropping, and creating the ad itself. If you just have the graphic of the book cover and a photo of you, you'll need to get something drawn up for the book. The two images do not make an ad. An ad needs graphics, copy, and layout

Most publications will expect you do to do the majority of the work necessary to prepare the ad for print. Ask for the ad guidelines in advance because each magazine is different. Even things like the physical size of a half-page ad will change from publication to publication. You'll need to know all of this information in order to generate the ad.

A number of graphics packages can be used to prepare camera-ready art for an ad. Adobe Photoshop is one of the most common, albeit expensive packages out there. Of course, this software is not cheap, and you need to consider how often you'll use the software to determine if it's best for you to buy or have the ads prepared for you. If you opt to have an ad prepared for you, try to come up with a design that can be scaled accordingly. You'll need to use this ad for most of your marketing needs, and it might have to fit a number of different spaces. Camera-ready means that the final output is in a TIF, JPG or PDF output.

While advertising might be a new idea to writers, the lecture tour has long been a part of our country's literary tradition. Mark Twain, Emerson, Dickens, and Oscar Wilde all crossed America to deliver talks to audiences. All you need is a forum and a topic to join this crowd. When working by yourself or as part of a group effort, you can deliver lectures on a variety of subjects to generate book sales. You can actually make money while promoting your book as well. Some groups will want you to come and give a talk to them about writing or some special area of expertise that you might have. You'll need to consider if you're cut out for discussing yourself in such an open forum. Some authors have no problems with it, and others can't bear the thought of talking about themselves for an hour or more. If you are comfortable with talking to an audience, you'll need to start to consider what topics you feel good about speaking on. Not all people can talk about the mechanics of writing. They just sit down and to it.

I find it very difficult to sit down and talk about the process of my writing. I don't have a specific plan or idea when I start a book and that makes it a bit odd to try to explain that to stranger. I tend to throw tons of research into my mind and let it simmer for a while, like a homemade stew. Then when it's all meshed together, I start the writing process. I don't find it an easy thing to talk about, and I'm superstitious enough not to want to talk about the book I'm currently writing. I worry that if I talk too much about it, I'll become so enthralled with the idea that I'll never manage to get it down on paper.

What I have found that works is to talk about book promotions. Obviously, I've been fairly successful at that, since I was asked to write this book, but it's easier for me to explain a well-crafted marketing plan than it is to try to explain my creative process. I do plan out where I'm going to tour and what I'm going to do in terms of print advertising. These things are more logical to me, and I find that I can more readily communicate them to others.

Some aspects of writing are more clinical and I also find that I can write about them. For example, my method for selecting stories for mystery anthologies is another topic I'm often asked to talk about. Research is always fascinating in terms of what you come up with and how you can find ways to use it in the course of your work. Since I write historical mysteries and biographies, I can talk about research from the fiction and non-fiction points of view.

I find audiences who come to listen to a writer always want to hear about the untold secrets of how to get into print. No matter what I speak about for an hour, I can be sure that someone in the audience will ask for tips on how to get an agent, and how to find a publisher. Even if they have yet to put a word to paper. It's hard to try to maintain that balance between being positive and realistic in terms of what to tell these listeners. I always suggest that they start by writing the very best book possible, and then worry about the agent. Parents don't worry about the college their child will attend before they even start trying to have a baby. It just isn't done, and it shouldn't be done in writing either. You'll have to get used to these questions and come up with ready-made answers to them. It's very difficult to strike that balance on the spur of the moment.

Of course, there are other things in the world besides writing, and other topics that you can talk about. If your book has a particular theme or activity in it that you're knowledgeable in, you can speak about that subject as well. I get a number of offers to speak about the Civil War, and Grant. While I feel comfortable in talking about Grant, I don't feel intelligent enough to speak regarding the Civil War. There's so much to that topic that I just don't know. Be sure to know your topic intimately before you agree to talk about it. There's nothing worse than for the audience to realize they know more than the speaker does. It's not a good way to sell books.

It almost goes without saying, but I'll say it anyway, since this is the topic of this book! You should make arrangements to sell books at all of these functions. If no one involved with the coordination of the event can be available to sell books for you, then you should request a friend or a family member to handle the financial aspects of the evening. You could do it yourself, but you're likely to feel pressured if you're talking to people after the lecture while simultaneously making change for a sale. You should try to concentrate on making the sale while someone else handles the money. After all, that's what you're there for.

If you're not comfortable speaking before large groups of people, then you should think about writing articles on topics related to writing or areas where you feel comfortable being considered an expert or at least knowledgeable. There are a number of magazines that feature articles about writing: *Writer's Digest*, *The Writer*, and many others. By letting other people know that you're serious about your craft, you're implying that you are serious about what you've written. From that you've made an impression on many would-be writers.

In the same way that you researched topics and subjects to speak about for money, look into the different areas where you have expert knowledge. For example, while I can discuss the history of the mystery genre for a lecture, I can definitely present myself as an expert on Craig Rice. I'm also a black belt in tae kwon do, which allows me to teach this martial art. These areas will likely net you some new readers. By now, your marketing efforts should have made an impression on the people who are big fans of your genre. You should have your name out to them through conventions and Internet communities. Now you're looking to reach a broader audience in terms of sales. You're looking to get your name out to a variety of people. The more articles you can write, the more well-known your name will be in a number of circles. Not only is this a great marketing tool, but in most cases, your freelance writing work will net you some extra income.

Typically a magazine article will have a by-line and a brief biography. If they don't typically provide this, see if you can get them to make an exception for your piece. Make sure to include your book title in that biography. "Jeff Marks is the author of *Gone With the Wind*, and lives in Cincinnati." Suddenly, you've opened your promotions to a whole new audience. It's much cheaper than advertising in the magazine, and you're also giving the reader a small taste of your writing style as well. They'll know if it's something they might like from reading your article.

Unlike 50 years ago, you're judged on each title and you need to make every book count. Everyone has a story (or stories) to tell in her writing. It's a matter of being able to sell those stories in such a manner that will keep readers coming back and keep publishers wanting to put your books out on the market. It won't do you any good to write the world's best novel if you have a track record of not promoting your works.

If you've read to this point in the book and implemented the suggestions that I've laid out, you're well on your way to having a successful career in writing. You've learned the basics of marketing your book, and found some advanced techniques to increase your audience while you continue to produce high quality fiction. You should be proud of yourself. Not many people make it this far in the field. Keep it up and some day I'll be standing in line at your booksigning, looking for advice.

Appendix A – What You'll Need for Your Office

To implement all the suggestions, you'll need to have a decently equipped office. I find that people always want to know what I have in my arsenal in order to successfully market books. So I thought I would give everyone a list of the things that I find necessary to run my writing business.

- A good computer. One with at least a one terabyte hard drive, and a 23" monitor. Your processor should always be within one level of the top of the line. Right now, that would mean a Athlon II, Xeon, or Core 2.

- High-speed Internet access. I won't get into arguments about cable or DSL, but just get one. It's worth its weight in gold.

- A good word processing program. For most people that's going to be Microsoft Word. I'm not going to argue its monopoly on the market and whether that is good or bad, but it has label making and mail merge features, which you need.

- A good spreadsheet package that can integrate with your word processor. For storing contact information.

- A fax machine or fax software on your computer.

- A color printer that can handle printing photographs and can print duplex (both sides of a piece of paper).

- Copy machine. In many cases, you can buy a 3-in-1 machine, fax, copier and printer.

- Scanner. In many cases, you can buy one as part of your color printer.

- Software to run a blast fax service (download from your selected provider)

- E-mail access

- Web-design software

- FTP software (can pull this free from the Internet)

- Filing cabinets and file folders

- Good digital camera for booksignings and events.

- Bulk supplies from the local office supply store. Labels, paper, photo paper

- Bulk supplies from the packaging store. Mailing envelopes that accommodate 1 or 2 copies of your book, small boxes, 9"x13" mailing envelopes.

Appendix B Writers' Resources

Major Review Publications

Send galleys to the following:

Publisher's Weekly
Messenger address: 232 West 17th Street
New York, NY 10011

Mailing address: 245 West 17th Street
New York, NY 10011
Phone: (646) 746-6781
Fax: (646) 746-6631
www.publishersweekly.com

Follow-up: To enquire if galleys have
arrived and been assigned for review, e-mail them at
pwreviewstatus@reedbusiness.com .

Library Journal
Book Review Editor
360 Park Avenue South
New York, NY 10010
Phone: (646) 746-6818
Fax: (646) 746-6734
ljquery@reedbusiness.com
www.libraryjournal.com

Booklist
Adult books: Brad Hooper

American Library Association

50 East Huron Street

Chicago, IL 60611

Phone: (800) 545-2433

Fax: (312) 337-6787

bhooper@ala.org

www.booklistonline.com

Independent Publisher Online

1129 Woodmere Ave. Suite B
Traverse City, Mi 49686

Phone: (800) 706-4636

Fax: (231) 933-0448

www.independentpublisher.com

ForeWord

Managing review editor: Alex Moore

129 1/2 East Front Street

Traverse City, MI 49684

Phone: (231) 933-3699

Fax: (231) 933-3899

E-mail: annes@traverse.com

www.forewordmagazine.com

Kirkus Reviews

All adult titles: Eric Liebetrau
Kirkus Reviews
Nielsen Business Media
770 Broadway, 7th Floor
New York, NY 10003

Phone: (646) 654-5865

Fax: (646) 654-5518

Send *two* copies.

Follow-up: Mail a SASP.

Kirkusrev@Kirkusreviews.com

www.kirkusreviews.com

Choice

100 Riverview Center, Suite 298

Middletown, CT 06457-3445

Phone: (860) 347-6933

Fax: (860) 704-0465

submissions@ala-choice.org

www.ala.org

Send *only finished books.*

Chicago Tribune

Elizabeth Taylor, Literary Editor

435 North Michigan Avenue

Chicago3 IL 60611

Phone: (312) 222-3429

Fax: (312) 222-2598

www.chicagotribune.com

Christian Science Monitor

Attn: Marjorie Kehe

One Norway Street

Boston, MA 02115-3995

Phone: (617) 450-2372

Fax: (617) 450-2317

www.csmonitor.com

Houston Chronicle

801 Texas Ave.

Houston, TX 77002

Phone: (713) 220-7171

Fax: (713) 220-3575

www.chron.com

Los Angeles Times

202 West 1st Ave

Los Angeles, CA 90012

Phone: (213) 237-5000

Fax: (213) 237-4712

"Book Calendar" deadline: Two weeks before desired publication date.

For review consideration: Send galleys three months in advance

www.latimes.com

The Daily News (New York)

450 West 33rd Street

New York, NY 10001

Phone: (212) 210-2100

Fax: (212) 643-7828

www.nydailynews.com

The New York Times

Sam Tanenhaus, *Book Review* editor

229 West 43rd Street New York, NY 10036

Phone: (212) 556-1831

Fax: (212) 556-3690

thearts@nytimes.com

www.nytimes.com

Newsday

235 Pinelawn Road

Melville, NY 11747

Phone: (613) 843-2900

Fax: (516) 843-2065

www.newsday.com

Philadelphia Inquirer

400 North Broad Street

P.O. Box 8263

Philadelphia, PA 19101

Phone: (215) 854-4531

Fax: (215) 854-5884

www.philly.com

USA Today
Carol Memmott, Book Editor
7950 Jones Branch Drive

McLean, VA 22108

Phone: (703) 854-6001

Fax: (703) 854-2030

cmemmott@usatoday.com

www.usatoday.com

The Wall Street Journal
Robert Messenger, Book Editor
200 Liberty Street
New York, NY 10281
Guidelines: (212) 416-3512

Fax: (212) 416-2658

www.wsj.com

The Washington Post
Marie Arana, *Book World* editor
1150 15th Street, NW
Washington, DC 20071
Phone: (202) 334-7470

Fax: (202) 334- 5269

Guidelines: (202) 334-4855

bookworld@washpost.com

www.washingtonpost.com

Mystery Scene
331 West 57th Street
Suite 148
New York, NY 10019-3101

Founded in 1985, Mystery Scene covers the crime and mystery genre with articles, essays, reviews and interviews.

Small press books should be addressed to the small press columnist.

www.mysteryscenemag.com

Selected Newswire Services

The Associated Press/AP

50 Rockefeller Plaza, 5th Floor

New York, NY 10020

Phone: (212) 621-1500

Fax: (212) 621-1679

www.ap.org

Copley News Service

350 Camino de la Reina, P.O. Box 191
San Diego, CA 92112-4106
Phone: (619) 299-3131

Fax: (619) 293-2322

www.copleynews.com

Bloomberg Business News

499 Park Avenue, 15th Floor

New York, NY 10022

Phone: (212) 318-2000

Fax: (212) 980-2480

www.bloomberg.com

Gannett News Service

Headquarters
7950 Jones Branch Drive

McLean, VA 22107
Phone: (703) 854-6000

Fax: (703) 854-2152

www.gannett.com

Knight-Rider Newspapers

700 National Press Building

Washington, DC 20045

Phone: (202) 383-6000

Fax: (202) 383-6075

Reuters America, Inc.

1333 H Street, NW, #410

Washington, DC 20005

Phone: (646) 223 6100

E-mail: editor@reuters.com

www.reuters.com

Press releases are only considered in electronic format and are reviewed before being sent out on the news wire.

Scripps Howard News Service

1090 Vermont Ave. N.W. Suite 1000

Washington, D.C. USA 20005
Phone: (202) 408-1484

Fax: .(202) 408-5950

www.shns.com

UPI/United Press International

Headquarters
1510 H Street, NW
Washington, DC 20005
Phone:(202) 898-8000
FAX:.(202) 898-8057

www.upi.com

Sales/Distribution Networks

Midpoint Trade

27 West 20th Street, Suite 1102

New York, NY 10011

Phone: (212) 727-0190

Fax: (212) 727-0195

info@midpt.com

www.midpointtrade.com

National Book Network

4501 Forbes Blvd., Suite 200
Lanham, MD 20706

Phone: (301) 459-3366
Fax: (301) 429-5746

www.nbnbooks.com

Wholesalers / Distributors

Baker & Taylor Books

1120 Rte 22 E

Bridgewater, NJ 08807

Phone: (800) 775-1500

Phone: (908) 541-7000

www.btol.com

Ingram Book Company

One Ingram Blvd

LaVergne, TN 37086

Phone: (800) 937-8000

Phone: (800) 937-8200 (stock availability through Access)

www.ingrambook.com

Biblio

4501 Forbes Blvd., Suite 200
Lanham, MD 20706
Phone (301) 459-3366
Fax (301) 429-5746

www.bibliodistribution.com

Book Clearinghouse

46 Purdy Street
Harrison, New York 10528
Phone: (914) 835-0015
Fax: (914) 835-0398
www.bookch.com

Partners Book Distributing, Inc.

2325 Jarkco Drive

Holt, MI 48842

Phone: (517) 694-3205

Phone: (800) 563-2385

Publishers Group West (PGW)

1700 4th Street

Berkeley, CA 94710

Phone: (800) 788-3123, (510) 809-3700

Fax: (510) 528-3444

www.pgw.com

Quality Books

1003 W. Pines Rd

Oregon, IL 61061kick

Phone: (815) 732-4450

Fax: (815) 732-4499

www.quality-books.com

Unique Books

5010 Kemper Ave

St. Louis, MO 63139

Phone: (314) 776-6695

www.uniquebooksinc.com

Associated Publishers Group

1501 County Hospital Rd

Nashville, TN 37218

Phone: (615) 254-2450

Fax: (615) 254-2405

www.apgbooks.com

National Book Network

4720 Boston Way

Lanham, MD 20706

Phone: (800) 462-6420

Fax: (301) 429-5746

www.nbnbooks.com

Bookstore Chains

Barnes &Noble

122 Fifth Avenue

New York, NY 10011

Phone: (212) 633-3454

Fax: (212) 677-1634

www.bn.com

Books-A-Million

402 Industrial Lane

Birmingham, AL 35211-4465

Phone: (205) 942-3737

www.booksamillion.com

Indigo Books and Music Inc (formerly Chapters of Canada)

Jim Hart, New Vendor Liaison

90 Ronson Drive

Etobicoke, Ontario M9W iCi

Phone: (416) 243-3138

Fax: (416) 243-8964

www.chapters.indigo.ca

Airport Bookstores

WH Smith

3200 Windy Hill Road, #1500

West Atlanta, GA 30339

Phone: (770) 952-0705, (404) 765-9480

www.whsmith.co.uk

Paradies Shops

5950 Fulton Industrial Boulevard

P.O. Box 43485

Atlanta, GA 30336

Phone: (404) 344-7905

www.theparadiesshops.com

On-Line Bookstores

Amazon Books

1200 12th Street S

Seattle, WA 98144

Phone: (206) 622-2335

www.amazon.com

Barnes &Noble

122 Fifth Avenue

New York, NY 10011

Phone: (212) 633-3454

Fax: (212) 677-1634

www.bn.com

Book Sense

Independent Booksellers Online

828 S Broadway

Tarrytown, NY 10391

Phone: (800) 637-0037

www.booksense.com

Book Clubs

Book Span

Bertelsmann Direct North America
One Penn Plaza
250 West 34th St., 5th floor
New York, NY 10119
212 930-4531

www.bookspan.com

Mystery Guild is a part of Book Span, Inc.

Literary Guild of America

Bantam Doubleday Dell

1540 Broadway

New York, NY 10036

Phone: (212) 782-7253

www.booksonline.com

Conservative Book Club

One Massachusetts Ave. NW

Washington DC 20001

Phone: (202) 216-0601

Fax: (202) 216-0614

www.eaglepub.com

Selected Catalogs

Miles Kimball
41 West 8th Avenue
Oshkosh, WI 54901
Phone: (414) 231-3800
Fax: (414) 231-4804
www.mileskimball.com

National Syndications
230 Fifth Avenue
New York, NY 10001
Phone: (212) 686-8680

Publisher's Clearinghouse
382 Channel Drive
Port Washington, NY 11050
Phone: (516) 883-5432
Fax: (516) 767-3650
www.pch.com

Signals
1000 Westgate Drive
St. Paul, MN 55164-0422
Phone: (612) 659-3700
www.signals.com

Lillian Vernon
One Theall
Rye, NY 10580
Phone: (914) 925-1200
Fax: (914) 925-1444
www.lillianvernon.com

Shop at Home,

Belcaro Group

7100 E Belleview Avenue #208,

Greenwood Village CO 80111;

(303) 843-0302; (800) 315-1995

Fax: 303-843-0377.

Email: sales@belcarogroup.com

Premium/Incentive Trade Associations

Incentive Manufacturers & Representatives Aliance (IMRA)

1805 North Mill Street, Suite A

Naperville, IL 60563

Phone: (630) 369-3466

Fax: (630) 369-3773

e-mail contactus@incentivemarketing.org

www.incentivemarketing.org

Promotional Marketing Association of America (PMAA)

257 Park Avenue South, Suite 1102

New York, NY 10010

Phone: (212) 420-1100

Fax: (212) 533-7622

www.pmalink.org

Website Submission Aggregators

www.addme.com

My personal favorite of the aggregators, easy to use and flexible.

www.exploit.com

Use the site's Submission Wizard to load your site to all the major search engines.

Direct Mail List Services

ListBazaar.com

InfoUSA, Inc. 5711 South 86th Circle

P.O. Box 27347

Omaha, Nebraska 68127

Phone: (888) 438-LIST

Marketing@listbazaar.com

www.listbazaar.com

www.usps.com/directmail/welcome.htm

The U.S. Post Office's site for dealing with direct mail. The site has information on reducing the cost of a mailing by use of standard sizes, and pre-sorting options.

ThinkDirectMarketing.com

470 West Avenue

Stamford CT 06902

Phone: (203) 964-9411

Fax: (203) 978-5872

E-Mail:info@thinkdm.com

www.thinkdirectmarketing.com

Pitney Bowes Inc.

World Headquarters

1 Elmcroft Road

Stamford, CT 06926-0700

Phone: (800) 672-6937

www.pitneyworks.com

DM News

Editorial and Advertising Office

100 Avenue of the Americas

New York, NY 10013

Phone: (212) 925-7300

Fax: (212) 925-8752

www.dmnews.com

Great site for updates on direct mail theory and all the sites regarding lists, postage, mailings.

Open Horizons

Box 205

Fairfield, IA 52556

Phone: (800) 796-6130

Phone: 800-796-6130
Fax: 641-472-1560

E-mail: info@bookmarket.com

www.bookmarket.com

American Business Lists

5711 S 86th Cr

Omaha, NE 68127

Phone: (800) 336-8349

Phone: (402) 930 3500
Fax: (402) 331 0176

www.infousa.com

Para-Lists by Poynter

Box 8206

Santa Barbara, CA 93118

Phone: (805) 968-7277

Fax: (805) 968-1379

www.parapublishing.com

Specialty Advertising Materials

Best Impressions

Box 802

LaSalle, IL 61301

Phone: (800) 635-2378

www.bestimpressions.com

4Imprint

Phone: (877)-4IM-PRINT

Fax: (800) 355-5043

www.4imprint.com

Postcard, Business Card, and Bookmark Production

www.allgraphicdesign.com/templates.html

Choose from a variety of templates to mail out postcards quickly.

Modern Postcard
1675 Faraday Avenue

Carlsbad, CA 92008

Phone: (760) 431-7084, (800) 959-8365

Fax: (760) 431-1939

www.modernpostcard.com

Postcard Press

16147 Wyandotte Street

Van Nuys, CA 91406

Phone: (800) 957-5787

Fax: (818) 909-7555

E-mail: postcard@pacbell.net

www.postcardpress.com

Vista Print
www.vistaprint.com

Home Shopping Networks

QVC Network-Vendor Relations

Mail Stop 0846 Studio Park,

West Chester, PA 19380

Phone: (610) 701-8894, (610) 701-1154, (610) 701-8655

Fax: (610) 701-1356

(They refuse to publicly release the name of their book buyer.) Request a Vendor Relations package or go online at www.QVC.com and download Vendor Information.

Home Shopping Network

Purchasing Department

1 HDSN Drive St.

Petersburg, FL 33726

Book buyer: Sarah Hawkins

Phone: (813) 572-8585, ext. 4066

Fax: (813) 573-3702

Call (800) 436-1010 for a Vendor Information Kit.

Promotional Products Association International (PPA)

3125 Skyway Circle

North Irving, TX 75038

Phone: 972-252-0404

Fax: 972:258-3004

www.ppa.org

ValueVision-International

6740 Shady Oak Road

 Eden Prairie, MN 55344

 Phone: 612-947-5200

Book buyer: Lori Griggs (purchasing)

Phone: 612-831-0166 (purchasing)

Fax: 612-947-0188 (corporate)

They do not provide forms or kits. You must take the initiative and mail or fax: data profile, cost, suggested price, brochure, pictures, catalog, etc.

Shop at Home, Inc.

P0 Box 12600

Knoxville, TN 37912

Book buyer: Henry Shapiro, vice President of Merchandise

Phone: 423-688-0300

Fax: 423-687-7166

Fax them your fax number, address, and phone. They will reply with a simple one-page New Vendor Inquiry Form.

Specialty Booklet Printers

Kirkland Offset Printing

Jerry Kirkland

7401 Princess View Drive, Suite F

San Diego, CA 92120

Phone: (619) 583-3676

Fax: (619) 583-3887

www.kirklandprinting.net

Sterling Pierce

William Burke

422 Atlantic Avenue

East Rockaway, NY 11518

Phone: (516) 593-1170

Fax: (516) 593-1401

www.sterlingpierce.com

Triangle Printing Company

1000 E. Boundary Ave.

York, PA 17405
Phone: (717) 854-1521 •

Phone: 800-777-4872

www.triangle-printing.com

Books and Newsletters

Literary Market Place (LMP)

This directory of the publishing industry includes lists of publicists, publishers, agents, lecture agents, organizations, media and writer's conferences.

RR Bowker,

RENP – North Building

121 Chanlon Rd.,

New Providence, NJ 07974

Phone: (888) 269-5372

E-mail: info@bowker.com

www.bowker.com

Book Marketing and Publicity

Infocom Group

5900 Hollis St. Suite R2

Emeryville, CA 94608

Phone (510) 596-9300
Phone: (800) 959-1059

Fax (510) 596-9331

www.infocomgroup.com

Events

Literary Market Place and the May issues of *Writer's Digest* and *The Writer* magazines list writer's conferences.

PMA Publishing University held the two days before BEA begins.

Publishers Marketing Association,

627 Aviation Way

Manhattan Beach, CA 90266

Phone: (310) 372-2732

Fax: (310) 374-3342

E-mail: info@pma-online.org

www.pma-online.org

Jeffrey Marks, author of this book, Intent to Sell

International speaker on marketing and book promotions

www.jeffreymarks.com

Media Directories

Bacon's Media Calendar Directory

Lists the lead editorial calendars of two hundred daily papers and 1,100 magazines. Important if your book's sales are keyed to a season or holiday. Includes a free bi-monthly newsletter.

Cision

332 S. Michigan Ave., Ste. 900,

Chicago, IL 60604

Phone: (800) 621-0561

www.bacons.com

Broadcasting Cable Yearbook

121 Chalon Rd.,

New Providence, NJ 07974

Phone: (888) 269-5372

Fax: (908) 771-7704

E-mail: info@bowker.com

Website: www.bowker.com

Gebbie Press

Box 1000

New Paltz, NY 12561

Phone: (845)255-7560

Fax: (845) 256-1239

Box 1000

New Paltz, NY 12561

Phone: (845)255-7560

Fax: (845) 256-1239

www.gebbieinc.com

Mark Gebbie provides links and e-mail addresses that will enable you to e-mail the media. Gebbie Press specializes in online promotion.

Burrelle's Media Directory

Burrelle's Information Systems,

75 E. Northfield Rd.,

Livingston, NJ 07039

Phone: (800) 631-1160

www.burrelles.com

Marketer's Guide to Media

Adweek Directories,

1515 Broadway,

New York, NY 10036

The Yellow Book Leadership Directories

104 Fifth Ave.,

New York, NY 10011

Phone: (212) 627-4140

www.leadershipdirectories.com has media and industry news.

Mailing List Management

www.authorsden.com

Site that helps to promote authors and put them in touch with readers.

www.constantcontact.com

E-mail marketing software and mailing list management

www.VerticalResponse.com

Create newsletters and manages distribution lists.

www.yourmailinglistprovider.com

includes a pared down free version which can send 1,000 e-mails a day

Broadcast / Blast Fax Services

Vision Lab.
100 boul. Alexis-Nihon, Suite 470,
Montréal, Québec, Canada
H4M 2N9

Tel.: +1-514-334-9998

Toll-free: 1-877-334-9998
Fax: +1-514-334-3389

www.faxmate.com

Ifaxbroadcaster.com

Stanford Global Link Corporation

4984 El Camino Real, Suite 1000

Los Altos, CA 94022

Phone: (888) 553-6888

Fax: (650) 237-0260

www.ifaxbroadcaster.com

VillageFax

VillageEDOCS, Inc.
14471 Chambers Road, Suite 105

Tustin, CA 92780

Phone: (714) 734-1030

Fax: (714) 734-1040

www.villagefax.com

Actual Software, Inc.

180 East Fifth Street

Suite 228

St. Paul MN 55101-1633

Phone: (651) 221-0894, (888) 540-5919

Fax: (651) 665-0840

www.broadcast-fax.com

TotalFax

Intelliquis International Inc.

352 West 12300 South Suite 300

Draper, Utah 84020

Phone: (801) 990-2600

Fax: (801) 990-2612

www.totalfax.net

World Fax Services, Inc.

3820 Northdale Blvd.

Suite 103-A

Tampa, FL 33624

Phone: (813) 961.7776 (888) 961-7776

Fax: (813) 264-0204

E-mail:info@worldfax.com

www.worldfax.com

EasyLink Services Corporation
33 Knightsbridge Road

Piscataway NJ 08854
Phone: (800) 624-5266

Fax: (732) 906-1008

E-mail: sales@easylink.com

www.easylink.com

Publicity Services

Bulldog Reporter
Lists for different categories.
Infocom Group,
1250 *45th* St., #200,
Emeryville, CA 94608
Phone: (800) 959-4331
Fax: (510) 879-4331
E-mail: info@infocomgroup.com
www.infocomgroup.com

PR Newswire
Sends news releases to targeted or all media nationally and internationally.
Harborside Financial Center,
806 Plaza 3,
Jersey City, NJ 07311
Phone: (800) 832-5522
www.prnewswire.com

Publicity Blitz Media Directory-on Disk
More than twenty thousand print and broadcast contacts in more than seventy-three categories on disk or labels or in a report. Free catalog of lists, databases and publicity resources.

For more info and a free sample issue, send a fax to 610-259-5032 or call 1-800-989-1400, ext. 432.

QuickSilver Database
Seventeen thousand publicity contacts
Jenkins Group,
400 W. Front St.,
Traverse City, MI 49684
Phone: (251) 933-0445, (800) 706-4636

E-mail: jenkinsgroup@bookpublishing.com

www.bookpublishing.com

Talk Show Selects

Broadcast Interview Source

2233 Wisconsin Ave., NW

Washington, DC 20007

(800) 955-0311.

Fax: (202) 342-5411.

Email: editor@yearbooknews.com.

http://www.yearbooknews.com.

Press Clipping Services

Google Alerts

www.google.com/alerts

Online Review Sites

http://www.absolutewrite.com

Absolute Write

http://www.kindleboards.com

Kindle Boards for Kindle titles

http://www.nookboards.com/forum

Nook Boards, the forum has review boards

http://www.authonomy.com

Authonomy from HarperCollins

http://www.writersbeat.com

The Writer's Beat forums

http://www.goodreads.com

Goodreads is a site that has widgets for listing what you're currently reading and a link-in to Facebook as well.

http://www.mobileread.com

Mobile Read Forums

http://www.Librarything.com

Similar to Goodreads, Library Thing allows readers to list their books, review them and talk to other readers.

http://www.Redroom.com

Red Room, where the writers are

http://www.kindleobsessed.com/

http://novelcritic.com

Novel Critic is resources and advice for writers

http://www.writingforums.org

Creative Writing Forums

http://thebooxreview.com/about

The Boox Review aims to bring objective, comprehensive reviews of books and ebooks.

http://www.bestsellersworld.com/

Best Sellers World

http://blogcritics.org/books/

Blog Critics

http://www.theindiespotlight.com/

The Indie Spotlight

Online Resources

Book Group Expo

An organization of interest to authors who wish to speak to book groups around the country

849 Almar, C-175

Santa Cruz, CA 95060

Phone: 408-821-2967

www.bookgroupexpo.com

www.booktalk.com

Booktalk has an archive of articles about publishing, agents, authors and links to other sites.

www.bookwire.com

Book industry portal that is owned by RR Bowker.

www.booktv.org

Site for BookTV, the show sponsored by CSPAN-2.

www.AmericanWriters.org

Site for the American Writers series from BookTV and CSPAN-2.

www.murdermustadvertise.com

website that includes articles regarding book deals, book sales, and promotion

www.nciba.com

The Northern California Independent Booksellers

www.ralan.com

Ralan Conley's SpecFic and Humor Webstravaganza has information on humor and sci-fi markets, and six hundred writing links.

www.writersdigest.com

Includes daily publishing news, information about promotion and writer's conferences.

www.zinebook.com

Chip Rowe's *Book of Zines* provides info about 'zines and a network of 'zine editors.

Publicity Organizations

American Marketing Association
250 S. Wacker Dr., Suite 2000,

Chicago, IL 60606-5819

Phone: (312) 648-0536

Fax: (312) 993-7542

E-mail: info@ama.org

www.ama.org

Book Publicists of Southern California

6464 Sunset Blvd., Room 580,

Hollywood, CA 90028

Phone: (323) 461-3921

Fax: (323) 461-0917

www.bookpublicists.org

Northern California Book Publicity & Marketing Association (NCBPMA)

P.O. Box 192803,

San Francisco, CA 94119-2803

www.ncbpma.org

Public Relations Society of America (PRSA)

33 Irving Pt., New York, NY 10003

Phone: (212) 995-2230

Fax: (212) 995-0757

www.prsa.org

Has chapters, a newsletter and a directory. Website has a listing of all media for a given location.

Publication Services Guild (PSG)

PO Box 720082,

Atlanta, GA 30358-2082
Phone: (404) 874-1901

www.professionalspeakersguild.com

Publishers Advertising and Marketing Association

c/o Cathy Collins,

The Crown Publishing Group

201 E 50 St,

New York, NY 10022

Fax: (212) 333-5374

www.pama-ny.org

Publishers Association of the South (PAS)

Box 43533,

Birmingham, AL 35243

Phone: (205) 967-4387

Fax: (205) 967-0580

www.pubsouth.org

Publishers Marketing Association (PMA)

2401 Pacific Coast Hwy, Suite 102,

Hermosa Beach, CA 90254

Phone: (310) 372-2732

Fax: (310) 374-3342

E-mail: info@pma-on-line.org

www.pma-online.org

Publishers' Publicity Association Inc (PPA)

c/o Macmillan
866 Third Ave, New York, NY 10022
Phone: (212) 702-6757

www.publisherspublicity.org

Push Technology Vendors

RSS

www.create-rss.com

Digg It

http://tuggo.org/projects/diggit/

Writer's Organizations

The Academy of American Poets

584 Broadway Ste. 1208,

New York, NY 10012

Phone: (212) 274-0343

Fax: (212) 274-9427

E-mail: academy@dti.net

www.poets.org

Austin Writers League

1501 West Fifth St., Suite E2, Austin, TX 78703

Phone: *(512)* 499-8914   Fax: (512) 499-0441

E-mail: awl@writersleague.org

www.writersleague.org

Authors Guild

330 West 42nd St., New York, NY 10036

Literary Market Place

Phone: (212) 563-5904

Fax: (564) 8363

E-mail: staff@authorsguild.org

www.authorsguild.org

The Baker Street Irregulars
34 Pierson Ave.,

Norwood, NJ 07648

Phone: (201) 768-2241

E-mail: email@bakerstreetjournal.com

www.bakerstreetjournal.com

Organization dedicated to the study of the Sherlock Holmes canon

California Writers' Club

2214 Derby St., Berkeley, CA 94705

Phone: (510) 841-1217

www.calwriters.org

Christian Writers Guild

65287 Fern St.,

Hume, CA 93628

Phone: (559) 335-2333

Fax: (559) 335-2770

E-mail: nvrohrer@spiralcomm.net

www.christianwritersguild.com

Dog Writers' Association of America (DWAA)

173 Union Rd., Coatesville, PA 19320

Phone: (610) 384-2436

Fax: (610) 384-2471

E-mail: dwaa@dwaa.org

www.dwaa.org

Editorial Freelancers Association (EPA)

71 West 23rd St., Ste. 1504,

New York, NY 10010

Phone: (212) 929-5400

Fax: (212) 929-5439

www.the-efa.org

Garden Writers of America
10210 Leatherleaf Ct.,
Manassas, VA 20111
Phone: (703) 257-1032
Fax: (703) 257-0213
www.gardenwriters.org

Horror Writers Association (HWA)
P.O. Box 50577
Palo Alto, CA 94303
E-mail: hwa@horror.org
www.horror.org

International Association of Crime Writers
North P.O. Box 8674
New York, NY 10116-8674
Phone and Fax: (212) 243-8966
E-mail: mfrisquegc@apc.org

International Thriller Writers
P.O. Box 311
Eureka, CA 95502
membership@internationalthrillerwriters.com
www.thrillerwriters.org

The International Women's Writing Guild (IWWG)
P.O. Box 810
Gracie Station, New York, NY 10028-0082
Phone: (212) 737-7536
Fax: (212) 737-9469
E-mail: iwwg@iwwg.com
www.iwwg.com

Media Alliance
814 Mission St., Ste. 205,
San Francisco, CA 94103
Phone: (415)546-6334
Fax: (415)536-6218
E-mail: info@media-alliance.org
www.media-alliance.org

Mystery Writers of America (MWA)
17 East 47th St., 6th Floor
New York, NY 10017
Phone: (212) 888-8171
Fax: (212) 888-8107
www.mysterywriters.org

National Writers Association
3140 S. Peoria, Ste. 295
Aurora, CO 80014
Phone: (303) 841-0246
Fax: (303) 751-8593
www.nationalwriters.com

National Writers Union
113 University Place, 6th Floor,
New York, NY, 10003-4527
Fax: (212) 254-0673
Phone: (212) 254-0279
E-mail: nwu@nwu.org
www.nwu.org

PEN New England (Poets, Playwrights, Essayists, Novelists)
568 Broadway, Ste. 401
New York, NY 10012
Phone: (212) 334-1660

Fax: (212) 334-2181

E-mail: pen@pen.org

www.pen.org

PEN Center USA West

672 S. Lafayette Park P1., Ste. 41,

Los Angeles, CA 90057

Phone: (213) 365-8500

Fax: (213) 365-9616

E-mail: pen@pen-usa-west.org

www.pen-usa-west.org

Poets & Writers

72 Spring St.

New York, NY 10012

Phone: (212) 226-3586

Fax: (212) 226-2963

www.pw.org

Romance Writers of America (RWA)

3707 FM 1960 West, Ste. 555

Houston, TX 77068

Phone: (281) 440-6885

Fax: (281) 440-7510

E-mail: info@rwanational.com

www.rwanational.com

Science Fiction & Fantasy Writers of America (SFWA)

P.O. Box 171,

Unity, ME 04988-0171

Phone and Fax: (207) 861-8078

E-mail: execdir@sfwa.org

www.sfwa.org

Sisters in Crime
P.O. Box 442124
Lawrence KS 66044
sinc@sistersincrime.org
www.sistersincrime.org

Society of Children's Book Writers & Illustrators (SCBWI)
8271 Beverly Blvd.
Los Angeles, CA 90048
Phone: (323) 782-1010
Fax: (323) 782-1892
E-mail: membership@scbwi.org
www.scbwi.org

The Society of Southwestern Authors (SSA)
P.O. Box 30355
Tucson, AZ 85751-0355
Phone: (520) 296-5299
Fax: (520) 296-0409
E-mail: wporter2o2@aol.com

Space Coast Writers Guild, Inc, (SCWG)
Box 804
Melbourne, FL 32902
Phone and Fax: (407) 727-0051

Western Writers of America
1012 Fair St.
Franklin, TN 37064
Phone and Fax: (615) 791-1444
E-mail: tncrutch@aol.com
www.wwa.com/home.html

Women's National Book Association (WNBA)

160 Fifth Avenue

New York, NY 10010

Phone: (212) 675-7804

Fax: (212) 989-7542

E-mail: skpassoc@cwixmail.com

www.bookbuzz.com/wnba.htm

Organizations Of Interest To Writers

American Booksellers Association

828 5. Broadway, Ste. 625

Tarrytown, NY 10591

Phone: (914) 591-2665 (800) 209-4575

Fax: (914) 591-2720

E-mail: editorial@bookweb.org

www.bookweb.org

American Library Association (ALA)

Public Information Officer

50 E. Huron St.

Chicago, IL 60611

Phone: (312) 944-6780

Fax: (312) 944-8741

www.ala.org

WorldCat

Catalog of Libraries

OCLC

6565 Frantz Road

Dublin OH USA 43017-3395

www.oclc.org/worldcat

BookExpo America (BEA)

383 Main Ave.,

Norwalk, CT 06851

Phone: (203) 840-2840

Fax: (203) 840-9614

E-mail: inquiry@bookexpo.reedexpo.com

www.bookexpo.reedexpo.com

The Center for the Book in the Library of Congress

The Library of Congress

101 Independence Ave, SE,

Washington, DC 20540-4920

Phone: (202) 707-5221

Fax: (202) 707-0267

E-mail: cfbook@loc.gov

www.loc.gov/loc/cfbook

Friends of Libraries USA

1420 Walnut St., Ste. 450,

Philadelphia, PA 19102-4017

Phone: (215) 790-1674 (800) 936-5872

Fax: (215) 545-3821

folusa@libertynet.org

www.folusa.com

Responsible for the library groups that typically order an author's books for a signing.

Independent Mystery Booksellers Association

 C/O Maryelizabeth Hart

Mysterious Galaxy

7051 Clairemont Mesa Blvd #302

San Diego, CA 92111

www.mysterybooksellers.com

Mid-Atlantic Booksellers Association

108 S 13 St,

Philadelphia, PA 19107

Phone: (215) 725-9598

Fax: (215) 735-2670

www.midatlanticbookpublishers.com

New England Booksellers Association Inc (NEBA)

45 Newbury St, Suite 506,

Boston, MA 02116

Phone: (617) 421-9340

Fax: (617) 421-9341

www.newenglandbooks.org

Pacific Northwest Booksellers Association
11510 Mill St,

Eugene, OR 97401-4258
Phone: (503) 683-4363

www.pnba.org

Small Press Center

20 W 44 St,

New York, NY 10036
Phone: (212) 764-7021

Fax: (212) 354-5365

www.smallpress.org

Small Publishers Association of North America

Box 1306

Buena Vista, CO 81211

Phone: (719) 395-4790

www.spannet.org

Southeast Booksellers Association (SEBA)

3806 Yale Ave,

Columbia, SC 29205

Phone: (803) 252-7755; (800) 331-9617

Fax: (803) 252-7879

www.sebaweb.org

Trade Show Bureau

1660 Lincoln St, Suite 2080,

Denver, CO 80264
Phone: (303) 860-7626

Fax: (303) 860-7479

Upper Midwest Booksellers Association (UMBA)
4018 W 65 St,

Edina, MN 55435

Phone: (612) 926-4102, 922-0076

Fax: (612) 925-5876

www.abookaday.com

Speakers Organizations

Dale Carnegie and Associates

1475 Franklin Ave.

Garden City, NY 11530

Phone: (800) 231-5800

www.dalecarnegie.com

National Speakers Association

1500 5. Priest Dr.,

Tempe, AZ 85821

Phone: (480) 968-2552

Fax: (480) 968-0911

www.nsaspeaker.com

Toastmasters International

23182 Arroyo Vista,

Santa Margarita, CA 92688-2620

Phone: (949) *858-8255*

Fax: (949) 858-1207

E-mail: tminfo@toastmasters.org

www.toastmasters.org

www.speakersdirect.com

The first online marketplace for speakers.

Speakers Network

1440 Newport Avenue,

San Jose, CA 95125

www.speakernetnews.com

A free weekly newsletter aimed at speakers that also provides valuable ideas for writers.

ABOUT THE AUTHOR

Jeffrey Marks is a long-time mystery fan and freelancer. After numerous mystery author profiles, he chose to chronicle the short but full life of mystery writer Craig Rice.

That biography (*Who Was That Lady?*) encouraged him to write mystery fiction. His works include *Atomic Renaissance: Women Mystery Writers of the 1940s/1950s*, and a biography of mystery author and critic Anthony Boucher entitled *Anthony Boucher*. It was nominated for an Agatha and fittingly, won an Anthony.

He is the long-time moderator of MurderMustAdvertise, an on-line discussion group dedicated to book marketing and public relations. He is the author of *Intent to Sell: Marketing the Genre Novel*, the only how-to book for promoting genre fiction.

His work has won a number of awards including the Barnes and Noble Prize and he was nominated for a Maxwell award (DWAA), an Edgar (MWA), three Agathas (Malice Domestic), two Macavity awards, and three Anthony awards (Bouchercon). Today, he writes from his home in Cincinnati, which he shares with his partner and two dogs.

Made in the USA
Lexington, KY
09 May 2013